PROFITABLE MAIL-ORDER MADE EASY

LAWPACK

Profitable Mail-Order Made Easy
by Garrett Adams

Copyright 1999 Law Pack Publishing Ltd

LAWPACK

10 - 16 Cole Street, London SE1 4YH
London SE1 4YH
www.lawpack.co.uk
All rights reserved.

Printed in Great Britain

ISBN 1 902646 46 0

Exclusion of liability and disclaimer

This publication is designed to provide accurate and authoritative information on the subject matter covered. It is sold on the understanding that neither the publisher nor author is engaged in rendering legal, accounting, or other professional services. If legal advice or other expert assistance is required, the services of a competent professional should be sought.

Whilst every effort has been made to ensure that this Made Easy Guide provides accurate and expert guidance, it is impossible to predict all the circumstances in which it may be used. Accordingly, the publisher, author, distributor and retailer shall not be liable to any person or entity with respect to any loss or damage caused or alleged to be caused directly or indirectly by what is contained or left out of this Made Easy Guide.

Table of contents

Introduction to Profitable Mail-Order Made Easy™

Welcome to the world of mail-order!

Hundreds, even thousands, of pounds can come to you through the mail, every day, when you build up a successful mail-order business, and we're going to show you how to do it! You don't need complicated equipment, a lot of capital, or an expensive office to start with. But you do need determination, a place to work (your home will do fine for a beginning), and a good product.

Before you begin to sell anything, take a moment to think about the possibilities of mail-order. In order to hit the real jackpot, your mail-order business, whatever it is that you will eventually sell, must be well planned, timely, and draw lots of repeat business. You are going to have to look at what other mail-order operators are selling, to see what kinds of products sell well, week after week, in the kinds of publications that you too are thinking of running ads in. And, don't forget to check back issues of these same publications to check out which ads stopped running, which products flopped!

Remember that the better prepared you are before you actually place your first ad, the better able you will be to cope with buying, selling, shipping and all the other new responsibilities you will have. But, don't let all this talk of responsibility scare you away—mail-order is still one of the least complicated ways to get set on the road to financial independence, and possibly great wealth!

Starting your mail-order business at home

1

Chapter 1

Starting your mail-order business at home

What you'll find in this chapter:

➤ What product should you sell?

➤ How to price your product

➤ Where and how to advertise your product

➤ The "big secret"

➤ How to test your results

How much money do you want to make? Do you need a steady second income? Do you want to have your own business, be your own boss, and make your own decisions?

Are you ready to make a commitment to be successful—both financially and personally? The mail-order business is the way to succeed. Whether you seek to commit a small amount or all your time, and if you want the satisfaction of being in charge, financial security, or social respect, the mail-order business is for you.

Today there are hundreds of opportunities to get into the profitable mail-order business. You don't have to be creative, clever, or have invented something new. You only need the determination to achieve your goals.

What do you want from life? Are you tired of struggling to make ends meet? Maybe you're fed-up with commuting to work and living under a time clock. If you like independence, can make simple decisions easily and are prepared to devote energy to your project, **you will succeed**.

The mail-order business is not a get-rich-quick scheme. It won't make you a millionaire overnight. But it can build into a steady, profitable business at home—as big or as small as you want it to be.

Some of the mail-order companies that gross millions of pounds a year got started in small ways. Not only the well-known distributors such as Past Times or Hawksmoor clothing, but dozens of smaller catalogue houses and monthly mail-order clubs began slowly, testing ads, testing prices, acquiring customers that buy again and again as each year passes.

Think big and think with confidence. The only way to truly make a mail-order business work is to make it work for you. This is a low risk, low investment business that can return you high profits.

Seize the opportunity

note Decide how much you want to earn, how much energy you can devote to this business, and what you want out of it. You can operate a successful mail-order business in your spare time with a very small financial investment, but it's up to you to make it work.

It is a proven fact that dozens of small and large companies make great profits from the mail-order business. Think about what you receive in the mail. Almost every day you get flyers and brochures from all sorts of companies selling magazines, books, clothing, household items—even holiday packages. Some you may toss away without even looking at; some of them you may read; and some you may buy from, especially if you know the company and have bought before.

An honest mail-order business is something to feel proud of. As valid as opening a shop on the high street, this business needs so little investment that, with perseverance, you almost can't help but win.

As in any other money-making enterprise, from working for someone else to owning and operating your own company, the mail-order business requires energy. But it doesn't take away enthusiasm or confidence. As a matter of fact, the more positive thought you put in, the more rewards you can reap.

What do you need?

You can run a small mail-order business out of your home from the kitchen table. All you really need is a mailing address, a few pounds for a classified ad, and a **product that sells.**

 If you're just starting in this business, you don't need to invest in elaborate equipment or expensive manufacturing. In fact, you may find several products to sell that require minimum investment and bring in a maximum profit.

Once you get going, you need the usual stationery supplies such as a stapler, cellophane tape, mailing envelopes, address labels, and file folders. You may invest in a file cabinet and a desk. And, you need to use a typewriter or computer or have somebody do all the typing for you.

Eventually you may need a franking machine, good quality postal scales, and storage areas for the products you sell. Even when you establish a high profit business, you can still operate it from a home with limited resources.

How to find what sells

 The basic secret to success in the mail-order business is to follow the leader. Especially when you're beginning, why should you spend the money and time to test products, prices, and places to advertise?

Start at your newsagent or library. Study every copy of each magazine that advertises mail-order products. Take a good look at the classifieds section. Write to dozens of these offers—especially any offer for something free. Take a look at the sales literature you get back. You may even purchase a few products to see what is sold for the money asked.

> **note**
> Consider the trends in the various magazines. You may notice several similar ads for the same products listed one after another. **They all sell.** That is where you should begin.

See the patterns?

If you review past issues of these magazines in the library, you'll notice the ads that repeat month after month. Advertisers who continue to place ads have **products that sell**. What are these products? Which ones would you like to promote?

What to sell

To be successful, you must offer something the others don't. It could be a unique product, your way of presenting the product, a new twist to an old product, something completely new, the best price—or any combination of these or other innovations.

Finally, you must find the right supplier. In the trade it is critical to deal only with a prime source—a manufacturer or direct importer (unless you can import yourself). Otherwise you will pay more for your products than your competition (a no-no). Small ads in the opportunity publication frequently attempt to appear as prime sources when they are not.

Some telltale indications of non-prime sources are: Use of an amateurish name, such as D&D Enterprises, the fact that others offer the same products, and the same wording used in ads with different addresses.

Manufactures of any size are listed in *Kelly's Manufacturers & Merchandise Directory*, found in your library. They can be checked out through a local Chamber of Commerce or through Dunn & Bradstreet, who will provide a basic report and rating service by telephone, for a minimal charge.

While you cannot be absolutely certain who advertises in opportunity magazines, check a trade journal for the subject, where the advertisers usually state whether they are a manufacturer, distributor or importer. Beware of those who import only one or two items and are middlemen for the rest.

Unless you have a product (something you do or make), look for something that is new, better, cheaper, more desirable or advantageous to the buyer than products by your competition.

Look through retail and wholesale advertisements for ideas of possible products and prices. Be careful not to pick something that is on its way out.

What products grab you? Which ones would you like to sell as a one-shot, and later as a product line? Maybe you already have a sound interest in specific products that are solid mail-order products, such as stamps and coins, jewelry or books.

Plans and kits are great to sell to decorating and handicraft publications. You may already make something at home for which you can easily write instructions and manufacture as an inexpensive kit for do-it-yourselfers.

Mail-order is an excellent way to distribute stock from a retail enterprise. If you have a store or manufacturing plant, you don't need to invest in stock. A simple brochure or catalogue to follow up inquiries is a profitable way to build business.

Specialised information is one of the most profitable products in the mail-order business. Whether you sell prerecorded cassettes or small folios or booklets, you can keep overhead down and profits high. Mass producing specialised information can be surprisingly inexpensive—and there's a high demand.

If you want to develop a product line, carefully research what already sells by mail-order ads. Don't take the chance to be innovative. Others have tried before you. Take the tried and true path and sell a competitive product at competitive prices in the same publications as everyone else.

There are a few rules to follow when choosing what to sell.

- Consider the profit margin. Don't work with anything that won't bear a high markup per item. Calculating the advertising costs, product costs and mailing, you have to make a good profit for each order.

Don't try to distribute novelties, gadgets or low-cost items through mail-order. The catalogue houses and other larger mail-order enterprises have that market covered.

- Consider the weight of the product and the mailability. Can you place it in a manila envelope and mail it? Padded mailers or small boxes are also easy to mail. Think twice about large or heavy items that are expensive to send.

- Is the product a regular in the publications? Do the other mail-order businesses carry this product? And does it sell profitably? Get some samples from competitors, then contact the manufacturers and find out about the profit margin.

- Can the product be sold in retail stores, and is it selling there? Unless the product is special, it won't maintain a high mail-order trade if it is readily available at the local stores.

- Do outside salespeople sell the product? Even if they are not sold in retail stores, steer away from items that are solicited for by telephone or personal sales calls. Also avoid any items that are distributed by persons from the manufacturing plants to smaller retail outlets.

- Is your product easy to advertise? In order to get inquiries through classifieds or display ads, you must be able to describe the product effectively with a few words. New inventions rarely sell well by mail-order.

note A basic element of the mail-order business is building repeat business. If you keep within a similar line of products, you can sell to the same customers time and again.

Finally, consider the potential of the product. If you begin with monogrammed bags, do you want to continue with an entire line of luggage, bags and cases? Where can you go after you have success with your first product? If you are producing and distributing information, what is the potential for more products on the same subject matter?

Eventually, you'll have distributed many similar products through mail-order. You may find one product to be a seller year after year and you may be content with that. Or, you may substitute your stock to improve the potential sales and actual profit. Think carefully about what type of product line you want to get into. You'll be living with it for a while, and you must have enthusiasm. Because it is through your product that your desires will be fulfiled and from which **you will make money.**

Your product

What's the least expensive way to produce your product and fulfil orders to make a high profit? If you are selling information, first test the market potential with photocopies of the report or booklet. Or, you may be able to revive an out of print publication.

If you want to distribute a product, contact several manufacturers that can make the merchandise and get competitive price quotations. Investigate ways to make the product with less expensive materials without losing quality. Check on the reputation of the firm. Is their merchandise known for quality? How soon can they deliver the goods once you have ordered?

You might try to sell a few handmade items first. Keep an adequate stock to fulfil orders, and consider mass production once the orders show the demand. Or, you can decide to work on consignment with somebody's product that is perhaps sold elsewhere. You try the product and make the sales. You get a percentage and the other people get a percentage. Then you work out a viable business relationship.

What price?

When you investigate the products you want to sell, consider the price you can get for them. Is there an adequate profit margin? How many times might a customer purchase your line of products in a one year period? Your profit line is the guide for deciding not only what to price your product at, but also the manufacturing costs and the feasibility of the product itself.

To test prices, you send sales literature with two prices. The results of the sales will tell you which is best. For example, if you get twice as many orders of a product at a lesser price, it will be a higher profit over a long run to keep it at the smaller price. However, if there is no big difference in the number of orders received, go for the higher price.

Consider the potential of your product and the product line. You'll want to expand into similar products and you'll want to make a tidy profit from the time you invest.

Where to advertise

Advertise where the competition is. If there is another classified with the same or similar product, place your ad in the same publication. Just as you followed the leaders in the choice and pricing of your product, follow the leaders in advertising.

> **TIP** For the first few months of testing, you may have to pay higher prices for the products in small quantities. Don't invest in large quantities until you are sure there is a demand.

Even though some publications cost more to place ads than others, don't try to save money in less expensive places to advertise. In the long run, your ad will pull the best responses where it's been tested and proven before.

There are two types of advertising for publications. Classified ads, which are run together in a section at the back of the publication are only for words, and usually are reasonably inexpensive to place. Display ads, or space ads, are the advertisements that run throughout the publication. They are best to use if you need to show a drawing of your product. Although they are more expensive than classifieds, your product response may do better with the extra investment.

Classified ads

Classified ads are the bread and butter winners for the mail-order business. Your investment per word in a classified will pull many pounds in responses.

The best way to use classifieds is with a two-part approach.

1) First you place a small ad that describes your product or service. You give a full address and information, but mention free details, or free information. Don't ask for money or give a price.

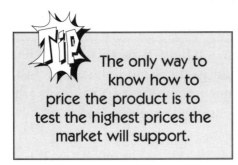
The only way to know how to price the product is to test the highest prices the market will support.

2) From the inquiries in response to the ad, send out a direct mail piece describing your product more fully—giving a full sales pitch and a coupon. It is this sales piece that is most effective in generating orders.

Writing classified ads is easy. Do what the others do. Read other classified ads.

First there is a lead-in, or headline—a word or two that grabs the reader's attention. This is followed by a promise—some benefit the product offers. Then comes the description of the product itself. Finally, offer a guarantee and push for action. Place the classified ad in the publications you choose under the categories that seem most effective for your product. Give it at least three months to test it. Then watch those inquiries turn into orders, and the orders turn into money.

Don't be tempted to place an ad in a magazine that does not have products similar to yours—even if you have a hunch or think it may bring in stray requests. For a beginner, follow the professionals and list where they do.

Display ads

If your product will sell better with a visual representation such as a line drawing or photograph, then you'll do best with a display ad.

Display ads come in all sizes—from one inch to a full two-page spread.

And choosing the size to run your ad will be a matter of testing the responses.

Whether it is the convenience or the simple indication of the type of information to include, mail-order businesses find that three-fourths of the orders from display ads will respond with the coupon.

As with a classified, use a catchy heading with the display ad to grab the reader's attention. Along with the illustration and coupon, describe the product and point out some of the benefits of owning it. And be sure to mention a guarantee.

You should use a space large enough to include a coupon. It has been proven that people respond faster if there is a space to fill out their name and address and place the order.

The rule of thumb for deciding how big to make the display ad is to test the responses. Increase the size of the ad until it costs more than the profits it brings in. Some products don't sell any better with a larger ad; others do.

Offer a refund

An important element in all advertising, and especially in mail-order, is to offer a refund if the customer is not satisfied. The reason is simple. More people will respond to an ad that backs up its claims with a guarantee.

If a buyer can return the product for a refund, then the order is a low risk. Since your product will fulfil the promises in the ad, you will have a low refund rate. For those returns you do have, fulfil the requests promptly. Just because that specific product was returned does not mean you lost a potential customer.

Use an address code

Whenever you place an advertisement, whether classified or display, you need to code the address so you know which ad the inquiry came from.

This coding system is called *keying the address*. Take a look at the classified ads you've been studying. See those codes? Department WD-5; Division 9A; Drawer 4B. These are all address keys to use in recording and tabulating responses. They are most important in testing the pull of your ads.

You can use any combination of letters and numbers to code the address. Most businesses use the words department, suite number, room number, division or drawer.

> *note* A simple key is the initials of the name of the publication and the number indicating the month of the issue. You can use any code that's easy to keep track of.

Direct mail

Once you receive inquiries from classified ads, and start fulfiling orders from display ads, follow up with direct mail pieces that sparkle with inviting offers.

Most mail pieces consist of a sales letter, a brochure or circular, and a reply card or coupon to cut out of the circular. Many people will respond directly to the product alone and order regardless of the sales literature. For the thousands of others who want to know more about what they're buying, you have to make the difference between throwing it away and sending in the coupon and a check.

The sales letter should be personal and direct. Talk to the potential buyer honestly, telling that person the virtues and benefits of the product. Point out the features and uses. And underscore the appeal for action.

Testimonials are effective ways of selling, especially if you need to convince the potential buyer of the actual results of the product. But be sure these can be backed up by real people who can make these claims.

Writing effective sales literature can be easy because it's standard. Look at all the other direct mail pieces you get. The same letter; the same brochure; the same reply card. These are the proven methods of selling by mail. Follow the experts and do the same.

> **note** The purpose of the two-step approach in classifieds is to get lists of potential buyers to sell to. Just as a salesperson gives a pitch with the product, you should also sell your offer with effective sales literature.

Start small. Use coloured paper to print up several hundred one piece circulars that describe your product and include a coupon. You don't have to create an elaborate four-colour photograph of the product; simply describe and illustrate the benefits and features of the offer.

In a few simple words, the buyer knows what the product is, understands that it is refundable, and expects to receive what is advertised. Direct mail pieces are the best way to follow up on your customer lists. Any inquiry you receive is a potential buyer regardless of any orders made. If your first mailing didn't spark a response, follow up with subsequent mailings.

You'll have to test to see how often these follow-ups are effective. Some mail-order enterprises mail offers several times a year; others only yearly catalogues.

The big secret

The BIG SECRET to a successful mail-order business is to sell more than one product.

note

The most expensive sale is the first one—because you had to FIND the customer. Now that you have him, sell him something else! Once you have accumulated a list of buyers for one product, they are good prospects for another product. They know you, you know them, and you know what they might be interested in!

Make an iron clad rule to NEVER send out a letter or package without an offer: don't waste anything! When you ship a gidget, enclose a flier for a "whatsit," and so forth.

If you don't hear from them, send a follow-up to the "whatsit," just like you did for the original product. Since your expenses are much lower for subsequent products, you have an

note Whether you use a one-piece circular, a full-colour brochure, or a forty-page catalogue, include an order coupon. The coupon is the most important piece in the direct mail literature. It makes it easy to place an order.

extra profit incentive to work on subsequent sales. Some mail-order dealers deliberately make **no profit** on the initial sale; they want the customer for subsequent sales!

Here is a sample checklist for going into the mail-order business:

1) Select a company name and make sure it isn't already being used by someone else.

2) Select a lead product and locate a reliable supplier.

3) Decide upon a business address and have headed paper printed.

4) Open a business bank account; it will take a years' trading before you'll be given the facility to process credit card payments.

5) Prepare a sales campaign: an ad, letter, flyer, coupon and return

envelope and have them printed. Do the same for follow-up correspondence.

6) Place test ads with a means to determine who answers which ad.

7) Send your letter and flyer to responders; keep careful records.

8) Send out follow-ups as needed.

9) Ship the product to customers, record the transaction on their "file" and include a flyer for another product.

10) Add the name to your buyer mailing list.

11) Repeat the ad (if it did well) or revise and try it in another paper. Repeat until you are satisfied with the results.

12) Expand to larger publications and bigger things.

One of the nicest things about the mail-order business is that there are so few rules. You can sell merchandise, your grandmother's recipes, books, courses, services or whatever—as long as you can match products with those who will buy them.

You can stay small or network with others by trading mailing lists and including each other's flyers in your mailings, or even selling each other's products on commission.

Eventually, you might consider including a freephone number in your ads, which may pay many times its cost in extra income. If you really get big, you can hire a company to handle your marketing.

Perhaps the most dangerous mistake beginners make in this business is underestimating the cost of selling.

If you pay £500 to mail out 1,000 advertisements and get a 5% return (50), the cost per response is £10. A £100 ad that pulls 50 queries means a cost per response of £1. Plan carefully and thoroughly—so you can enjoy a successful mail-order business.

Testing results

How do you know which ads pulled best? Which magazine gives you the best pound for pound response? What price is the most profitable to sell the product at? Which sales pitch works best? Keep a complete record of all the inquiries and orders, and make comparisons to determine the best roads to take.

note

One of the elements you need to test is the pull of the magazine ad. Compare each publication with the next. Which ones are the most profitable?

Testing is the hidden feature in mail-order that determines success. And testing doesn't need to be costly or draining to your profits. The best attitude towards testing is as a game.

Draw the limits of your risks and make different turns in the road when it isn't profitable. If you consider testing for mail-order like a maze, you'll be the one to find the success. One of the best features of the mail-order business is that it doesn't require a large financial investment.

So, each step of the way that you test, going ahead with high responses and discarding low response, you have little to lose and everything to gain.

If you are using display ads, you may be testing for which size pulls the best response for the money you invested. Another element that is tested is the ad copy—especially the headings. Test a few different headlines to see which is the most effective.

The obvious thing that is tested is the product itself.

Keeping records

The way to determine test results is with a record sheet. Use a separate sheet for each address key you used.

At the top of the paper, include the vital information such as the publication the ad was placed in; what type and size of ad was used; how much the ad cost; which ad copy was used; the name of the product; the price of the product.

note The most clever ad at the most appealing price will do nothing if the product won't sell. If your product is not successful, drop it and try something else. It's not worthwhile to put in so much effort for something that will never make it.

Separate the tabulations into two main categories: inquiries and orders. If you use a display ad, you should have fewer inquiries than directly from a classified, but you need to keep track of all responses.

Write consecutive numbers down the left-hand column. These will correspond directly to the days you received responses, starting with the first day you received an inquiry or order.

The inquiries section should be divided into three columns of date received, number received and a running total to keep track of how many to date.

The orders section should be divided into day received; daily number of orders; total number of orders; daily number of sales; and total cash sales. The totals give you an up-to-date indication of how well your ad is doing.

Create your own mail-order products

2

Chapter 2

Create your own mail-order products

Pick up almost any book or folio on mail-order selling and invariably you will find the same advice. When you select a mail-order product, select one which:

- Appeals to a large segment of the population

- Is not readily available in stores

- Is easy to ship by mail

- Is worthwhile

- Lends itself to repeat orders

Most mail-order writers will also tell you to try to acquire exclusive selling rights to your product. Most writers agree that a dealer has a better chance of succeeding in the mail-order business if he created the product himself.

All of this is certainly good advice. The trouble with it is that it does not go far enough. It does not tell you how to create a product that is exclusively your own. In what follows, I show you, step by step, how to create your own mail-order product.

I begin by making a very revolutionary statement. ***The first step on the road to mail-order success is not the selection of a product!*** That may sound like a very strange statement, but there are three things you must do (if you want to be successful) before you ever select a product to sell by mail!

1) Analyse yourself. You will only succeed in selling a product, or a line of mail-order products, if you really enjoy selling them, if you can be honestly enthusiastic about them, and if they are products you yourself would honestly want to buy.

2) Select your market. Once you analyse yourself, you will want to sell to people with interests similar to your own. Only then will you be comfortable in your mail-order business.

3) Analyse your market. Before you ever select a product, you should know what your market is buying, what it would like to buy, if available, and what it will buy from you, in the very near future.

Once you analyse yourself, select your market, and then thoroughly analyse your market, you will have no trouble selecting or creating a product to sell by mail. It will almost select you! Now, let's go back and study these three steps, one by one.

Analyse yourself

To help you understand yourself, sit down and, as honestly as possible, write out your answers to the following questions:

1) When I go to a newsagent, what kind of magazines appeal to me?

2) What kind of books do I really like to read?

3) When I daydream, what do I daydream about?

4) What do I do with my free time? (How do I spend my evenings? What do I do at the weekend?)

5) What do I do on my holiday?

6) What one subject interests me more than any other subject in the world?

7) If I didn't have to work for a living, how would I spend my time?

8) If I could go back to college, what subjects would I take?

9) What kind of products do I like to purchase by mail?

Once you honestly answer all these questions, you will see an amazing pattern emerging. When you finish, pay a visit to your local library. Go to the reference desk and ask to see the latest edition of the *Benn's Media*. Sit down and study the table of contents, which lists all the main categories of magazines currently being printed. Decide which category interests you beyond all others. It is in that mail-order market that you will be most at home. It is there that you will be most successful.

 Other publications that will prove useful by providing you with detailed information are:

• *British Rate & Data*

• *The Advertiser's Annual, Willings Press Guide*

• *Ulrich's International Periodical Directory*

For the sake of illustration, say that you have a compelling interest in astrology. With a little search in one of these directories, you will find the name and address of at least a dozen or so astrology magazines. In *Ulrich's* you will find even more, since it lists magazines published in foreign countries as well.

When you start receiving your sample copies, save them and save the advertising rate cards. They will be invaluable to you in the future.

Jot down the names and address of each and every publication. Write to each of them, on your letterhead if possible. If you don't have a letterhead, you will still hear from most of them. Tell them you are starting a mail-order business, specialising in astrological products, and ask them for a sample copy of their publications, along with their advertising rates.

If at all possible, try to find some old magazines, perhaps from a charity shop or second-hand bookseller. Get as many different magazine titles as possible and be sure to get copies with mail-order ads in them. Issues that are ten or fifteen years old will be valuable to you, but also try to obtain some of the more current issues. You are now ready to start.

Analysing your market

Start a notebook. Pick up one of the magazines and read the first ad. Read every line of it. Read it slowly and carefully. When you finish reading it, see if you can describe what is being sold in five words or less. If you can't, go back and read it again. If you can, record your description under one of three headings in your notebook:

- Merchandise
- Information
- Service

All mail-order offerings come under one of the three headings just listed. If the ad was for an aquarian necklace, it should be listed under merchandise. If it was for a treatise on flying saucers, it should be listed under information. If it was an offer to chart your horoscope, it should be listed under service.

After you analyse the first ad, study the next ad. Continue until you have thoroughly analysed every single ad in the magazine, including the classifieds. When you are through, you should have three lists:

1) A list of astrological merchandise for sale.

2) A list of astrological manuals (information) for sale.

3) A list of astrological services for sale.

As you read, watch for:

• **Undeveloped ideas**—especially in older issues, you will find really good ideas that were, for one reason or another, never developed. Perhaps the originator lost interest or didn't have the capital to develop his idea. He may have died or he may have run off with a dancer from a nightclub and forgotten all about the mail-order business. If you can develop the idea, you have a mail-order product.

note You will be amazed at what you will discover when you read magazines from the viewpoint of a mail-order dealer!

• **Wholesale sources**—watch for ads that say "dealers wanted" (in more current issues, of course). Here may be the perfect source of mail-order products for you.

• **The articles**—they show you what the readers are interested in and give you clues as to what the readers want to buy. Remember the articles are doing two things—they are about subjects which the readers are already interested, and they are also creating new interests in the minds of the readers. Can you create a product that readers will want as a result of reading those articles?

While researching this manuscript, I analysed two completely different magazines from the viewpoint of a mail-order dealer. I would like to share some of my findings with you. Don't worry that these references are all from American magazines. Nowadays, mail-order principles are the same for just about every market!

The first magazine I analysed was *Astrology—Your Daily Horoscope,* December 1975. I would like to begin with the merchandise offerings.

Astrology (merchandise)

The first ad is for personalised stationery. Any mail-order dealer knows you can sell personalised stationary to any market. This dealer took a commonplace product and adapted it to the astrological market. Next to the name and address which he prints on the stationary, he prints the astrological sun sign and he calls it zodiac stationary.

> *note* You'll be amazed at how you can turn commonplace items into red hot mail-order sellers just by taking the time to put yourself in your customer's shoes for a while.

The next ad is for another very common product—soap! You can buy soap in any grocery store. But, this soap is special. It has your zodiac sign imprinted in it, and it lasts as long as the soap lasts. Here is another good example of adapting a commonplace product to the special interests and desires of your prospective customers.

If you are now selling a product by mail and you would like to increase your sales, make a list of the kinds of people you would like to sell it to. (For example, doctors, waitresses, farmers, gun collectors, etc.) Then, go back and ask yourself what you could do to your product to make it appeal to each individual group.

The next merchandise offering is for "Seashells for Virgos and Scorpios." Had this advertiser offered plain old seashells in an astrology magazine, his mailbox would probably be empty. Had he advertised *"seashells for astrologers,"* he might have gotten a few orders. But he made his seashells special, exclusive, and very, very desirable, because they are only for Virgos and Scorpios. He is catching the attention of one reader out of every six and I would bet that ad was a mail-order success! Here is an idea worth remembering. Try to apply it to your product!

Another merchandise offering was a *"hand bio-rhythm computer."* For the past few years, astrology magazines ran article after article on the bio-rhythm theory (i.e. every male and female person has emotional, intellectual and physical cycles, which can be predicted in advance). The astrology magazines, in effect, created a mail-order market for this kind of new product. The ad promises, *"it reveals your emotional, intellectual and physical state— Even before the day begins!"* This dealer was clever enough to do something about this new interest. If he had not studied his market, he could never have discovered the need for a bio-rhythm computer!

Astrology (information)

Readers of astrology magazines are very interested in love, money, success, power, miracles, prayer, etc. One enterprising dealer wrote six "personal guidance" manuals, and runs full page ads in astrology magazines, selling them from $2.00 to $11.00 each! His ads have run successfully for years. Back in 1960, when I first became interested in selling by mail, this dealer was running small ads in mail dealer magazines, selling mail-order manuals!

Here are some of the other information manuals which dealers are selling by mail:

- How the Maya Indians foretold the future—$15.00

- Powerful words to be recited daily to end your money worries—$4.00

- How to spiritually heal your pets—$5.00

- A manual on etheric astral projection, written "especially for the neophyte"—$3.00

Can you create a worthwhile manual for this market? (I predict that the first dealer who writes a good manual on bio-rhythm will make a fortune!) If you need ideas for manuals, study the subjects being offered in the astrology magazines. Readers are interested in those subjects! This is only a partial list of articles I found about astrology:

- "Yearly Forecast for Sagittarius"

- "Basic Astronomy for the Astrologer"

- "Sybil Leek Analyses Your Dreams"

- "How to Make Your Dreams Pay"

- "How Mercury Inspires Your Creativity"

A study of old astrology magazines will provide you with a wealth of subjects for new mail-order manuals (or folios).

Astrology (service)

If there is one thing people who read astrology magazines love, it is this: They love to be analysed and counselled by professionals. Do you have specialised training in the art of horoscope reading? If so, you can sell your services by mail. Here are some of the headlines from ads offering such services:

- "Let an Expert Discuss Your Life!"

- "This Horoscope is About You"

- "Now—A serious study of you!"

- "Now there is a horoscope written for the two of you! One for you, one for your loved one! It could mean the difference between a happy marriage and a painful divorce!"

- "1999—2000—2001! Is one of these your year of destiny?" (this ran in an astrology magazine for at least ten years. Every year, the advertiser simply changes the dates!)

Other services being offered in this magazine include:

◆ personal questions answered by psychics and mystics

◆ spiritual readings

◆ tarot readings

◆ palm readings

◆ handwriting analysis

◆ questions answered through astro-extra sensory perception

Are you trained to offer such services through the mail? Or, are you interested in receiving such training? If your answer is yes, this is where you should begin your mail-order career.

The next magazine I analysed was the November 1975 issue of *Field and Stream*. Since this magazine is aimed at two mail-order markets, hunters and fishermen, I analysed only those ads pertaining to hunters.

Hunters (merchandise)

Men who hunt for wild game spend a lot of money on their hobby. They buy top quality hunting clothes. (who wants to go hunting in a cheap pair of jungle boots?) They spend a lot of money on their guns, their hunting knives, and on top quality binoculars. There are several dozen well-established mail-order companies selling this kind of merchandise to hunters. If you plan to establish a one-man mail-order operation, you would be well advised not to try to compete with these companies. Instead, look for something unique that a hunter can use, and begin your mail-order business there.

Here are a few merchandise offerings being made by enterprising dealers:

"Deer Hunter's Soap" (bathe in soap scented with the aroma of a female deer and you will attract a buck. Only $1.50 per bar!) Notice how a smart dealer adapted a commonplace item to a specialised market. Notice too that he adapted it to only one kind of hunter. He didn't offer it to bear hunters, to coon hunters, to quail hunters, or to game hunters in general. He offered it to deer hunters! If you are a deer hunter, you would notice that ad!

"Curtain Rods For Hunting Vans—$3.95 a pair." Sure, you can buy curtain rods in any dime store, but not curtain rods for hunting vans! Another excellent example of taking a commonplace item, adapting it to a specialised market, and creating a new mail-order product.

Also offered:

- gun cleaning cloths (10 for a dollar)
- brass nameplates for hunting dogs (not for just any old dog!)
- ID tags for your hunting dogs
- handwarmers and bodywarmers (boy, could you use these when you get lost in the snow!)

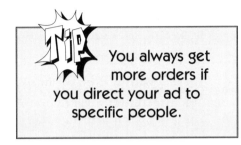

You always get more orders if you direct your ad to specific people.

There was a small classified ad offering "fish and game rubber stamps." I hope this dealer got a lot of orders, but if he didn't, I suspect it was because his offer was too general. First of all, it would have sold better with an illustrated display ad. Even better—Let us go back to the Virgo and Scorpio concept. How about rubber stamps for coon hunters? Or, for pheasant hunters? Or, rubber stamps for taxidermists?

Hunting (information)

Frankly, I was amazed at the amount of information folios being sold to hunters. Here are some examples:

- "How to Build Your Own Gun Cabinet"

- "Duck Calling Instructions" (30 minutes on tape!)

- "Chart showing life-size tracks of 38 animals in the Adirondack mountains."

- "How to Build Box Traps— $1.00"

A lot of information, in every field, is now being put on cassette tape and sold by mail. If you would rather talk than write, this could be an aspect of mail-order selling for you to consider.

- "My 50-year-old Secret to Racoon Trapping. Guaranteed, $1.00"

- "Mount Fish for Fun and Profit—Easy Instructions—$1.00"

- "Tan your own hides—hair on or off—complete, easy to follow instructions and formulas—$1.00"

- "Build (meat, fish, sausage) smoker! Inexpensive, portable—Easy plans, $1.00"

◆ "Wild game and fish recipes—deer, bear, rabbit, trout, salmon and dozens more—$1.00"

note incidentally, not all information is written. A lot of people buy plans, diagrams, etc. To digress, recently a dealer advertised plans to build your own flying saucer detector!

Can you write an information manual for hunters? Can you tell them how to shoot ducks? Or how to hunt buffalo? Or, what to do for snake bites? Or, how to sign up for a big game safari in the wilds of Africa? If you can, write a good manual (or put it on tape) and sell it by mail!

Hunting (service)

Unlike the readers of astrology magazines, game hunters don't give a damn about being analysed or counselled! But, if you can teach their hunting dog how to chase a bear up a tree, then they will probably pay you for your services. Can you repair their gun? Or, can you stuff and mount their catches? If so, you can build a mail-order business offering such services. .

In conclusion

Study your market thoroughly, and never stop studying it! Most successful mail-order people read dozens of magazines every month. They know what their customers are thinking about, what they need, and what they will buy.

Successful mail-order people are interested in the needs and wants of their customers first. They understand that if they concentrate on those, profits will flow naturally. Those who think only of profits soon pass by the wayside.

In the beginning of this manual, I asked you to write to every magazine in your chosen field. Subscribe to as many as possible. When you have created your first product, then start advertising in those magazines (which is why I said to keep their rate cards). Never run an ad unless you can run it in three consecutive issues. Then continue running it for as long as it continues to produce new customers for you. Slowly add new (but related) items to your line. Whenever possible, expand your business by inserting your ads in new publications.

Remember these simple guidelines:

- Don't copy anyone else!
  You are a unique individual. Express your own individuality in your mail-order business.

- Create something new and exciting!

- Create something useful and worthwhile!

- Create something you yourself would want to buy!

There are hundreds of mail-order markets for you to explore! Analyse yourself and then select the market that is best for you.

Basic steps to mail-order success

3

Chapter 3

Basic steps to mail-order success

What you'll find in this chapter:

➠ What you need to start

➠ Locating the right product

➠ Writing a successful ad

➠ Testing your ad

➠ Pricing your product correctly

The following is designed to provide a checklist for new entrants into the mail-order field. Each mail-order business is different, but there are common elements that apply to most mail-order businesses, as well as some specific characteristics that may vary from business to business. The following suggestions were developed to assist you in avoiding mistakes which can be costly. Apply the various points as they may relate to your specific business.

Company name and address

- Select a short, friendly, informal, easy-to-remember company name.

- Your personal name is acceptable, but add "Co.", "Gifts", etc.

- You may consider using a name that describes your product.

- Before spending money for printing material, make sure that the name you choose is not already registered to another company. Companies House will provide this information; the

note

Most newly established mail-order businesses operate out of a home until the volume of business requires larger space.

quickest way to find out is by using their website: www.companieshouse.gov.uk.

- Almost all publications will charge you a full word charge for each component of your address. Since advertising costs anywhere from ten pence to £10.00 per word (classified advertising) you could save a substantial amount of money at the end of the year if you keep your business name and address as short as possible.

Telephone

- Some mail-order companies do not show their telephone numbers on their stationery, others do. I believe it gives the customer some comfort to see a telephone number, although he may never use it.

- You can show your residence phone number in the appropriate printed material, or you can obtain a business listing for your home.

- If you plan to sell higher priced items (over £30.00), however, a business listing would be advantageous since a prospective customer may pick up the phone and check with the information operator whether "Company X" is listed.

Basic supplies

◆ Be conservative and frugal in your acquisition of items that you feel are needed. It's always wise to start small, and as inexpensively as possible. As you build profits, you can buy more and better items.

◆ A good quality typewriter or computer (you can rent one for starters for a few months).

◆ Neatly printed letterheads and envelopes. Business stationery, business envelopes and return envelopes are fine. All items should have your business name and address imprinted on them. You will also need some mailing labels and some miscellaneous office supplies.

Starting capital

You should have enough starting capital to pay for the following expenses:

• Starting supplies.

• Promotion expenses: ad placement in two or three publications to test your offer; preparation and layout of a display ad; art work and typesetting of circular; additional or continuing promotions if initial results are encouraging.

• Rental for a minimum of 1,000 names for a direct mail program, plus postage costs.

• Extra capital to allow for unforeseen and unexpected expenses.

Product

Select a product that, preferably:

♦ Is new, unusual and, if possible, exclusively yours; Is of good quality and fairly priced; Fills a definite need for a wide and ready market; Offers strong appeal to the prospect; Is not expensive to make or produce; Can be bought at low price; Interests a large percentage of the market; Lightweight; Not fragile; Safe and inexpensive to ship; Will be used up or consumed and must be reordered periodically.

♦ Is needed on an ongoing basis. Is not seasonable (except Christmas); can be sold the year around.

♦ Is of acceptable quality. Know the product before you sell it. You can control its production and/or distribution.

♦ Is not widely available from retailers. The more specialised your products are, the easier you marketing becomes. If you are selling books, for example, it would be impossible, except for a very large company, to sell all types of books. You may decide to specialise in books pertaining to sports, and may want to go even further by zeroing in on football or cricket.

> **TIP**
> Develop a line of merchandise. It is rarely possible to make money with just one or two items. The availability of a line of related products is paramount to mail-order success.

Locating a suitable mail-order item

• Look through mail-order sections of magazines to check what types of products successful mail-order dealers offer.

- Inquire of local manufacturers and Chambers of Commerce.

- Attend trade shows (with gift, jewelry, household themes, etc.)

- Contact appropriate manufacturers listed in Kelly's Manufacturers & Merchants Directory available at public libraries.

- Watch for new product listings in trade journals and magazines.

If you have a difficult time deciding what items or products to select, I suggest you read the book: *How Mail-Order Fortunes are Made* by Alfred Stern. This book lists hundreds of different items. It will give you many good ideas.

- Check out close-outs, surplus and overstock offers.

- Contact mail-order supply sources.

- Design, develop, manufacture or publish your own product.

The line

- Develop or acquire other items to tie in with your main product.

- Present follow-up offers to customers and prospects.

- Promote succession of products appealing to the same trade.

- Sell such services as p e r s o n a l i s a t i o n , consultation, etc., if such services are adaptable to your line.

Special interest products should be advertised in special interest publications. There are a number of quality mail-order publications, but it takes time to find the right publication for your product.

Suppliers

- Develop or produce your own mail-order item, if possible.

- Try to arrange exclusive mail-order rights with the supplier.

- Establish supply sources close to home to save delivery time and shipping costs.

- Seek lowest price if item is offered by two or more suppliers.

- Order larger quantities, if you can afford such purchases, to get lower prices or greater discounts.

- Ensure the supplier is reliable and will provide the merchandise you plan to promote; that he will ship orders promptly.

- Consider only products which allow an adequate profit margin (at least a 3 to 1 profit mark-up on lower-priced items).

- Your suppliers should provide you with reliability, quality, and reasonable pricing.

- Since you probably should provide some type of money back guarantee (30 days is standard), you should expect the same guarantee from your suppliers.

- When comparing suppliers, be sure to include their shipping charges in your calculations.

Pricing

- Use round numbers (£3.00, £5.00, etc.) for lower-priced items to make it convenient for customers to remit payment.

note Price merchandise fairly; give all customers their money's worth. Your prices of course have to be fair and in line with your competition.

- Test different prices to determine which selling price brings in the greatest amount of profit.

- Buy at a price that allows you an adequate mark-up. In setting your prices, allow for all costs: cost of product; shipping cost and postage; bank charges including credit card charges; wrapping; bad debts; rejects; refunds, etc. In addition, the other normal overhead costs need to be considered; marketing cost for advertising, and for printing of promotional items.

- The three biggest expense categories in mail-order are: advertising, printing cost, and postage. Over 80% of your total expenses are in this area. Watch these expenses very carefully.

Advertising

◆ Don't attempt to start unless you can afford at least two or three ads; or pay for a direct mailing to at least 1,000 names.

◆ Plan to advertise consistently.

◆ Use ad space relative to sale price, i.e., use small-size ads for low-priced items and larger ads for more expensive items.

◆ Items priced over £5.00 usually do not sell as profitably through classified ads.

◆ In space ads, offer products in the £5.00 to £15.00 price range.

◆ It is usually better to advertise for inquiries if an item sells for £10.00 or more.

◆ Two small ads generally produce more business than one ad twice as large.

◆ Repeat ads as long as they remain profitable.

◆ Don't waste unnecessary space; advertising is expensive.

◆ Don't expect to make a killing from one ad or mailing. Consistent advertising is the key to mail-order success.

Advertising expense

- Start with classified ads. As you test them and know what is successful, you can switch to display ads.

- To test an offering and a specific ad, run it once in a specific publication. You should get a reading that could be very positive or negative. It might also be inconclusive. If that is the case, simply run it again.

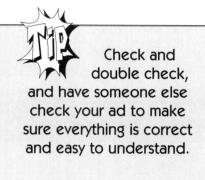

Check and double check, and have someone else check your ad to make sure everything is correct and easy to understand.

- It is best to test an ad by running it in different publications.

- Advertise in publications that advertise similar products.

- If you have a sure seller, buy larger space.

- Keep on changing the ad and offering it until you are satisfied it is right.

- Examples of changes you can make are: size of ad, copy, appeal, special gimmicks such as discounts, free gifts or reports, etc.

- Remember: An ad can be 20 or 30 times more successful than another ad advertising the same product. It pays, therefore, to continue testing until it is just right.

- Repeat a successful ad until you no longer get a satisfactory return.

- The conventional advertising cost is 15% of sales or more in mail-order.

- Be careful when you allocate advertising funds to small mail-order publications. The ad may appear to be very inexpensive. However, a £15.00 ad that gets no response is a lot more expensive than a £110.00 ad that gets over 100 inquiries.

> **note** Sales letters should have an attention getting opening. The idea of the opening is to get the customer to read the rest of the letter.

- Stay away from those publications that have no news or editorial content, and also those that have poor printing quality.

Advertising copy

- ◆ Use attention-getting, bold headline copy in ads.

- ◆ Illustrate the product if space permits; explain how it is used.

- ◆ Write tight copy.

- ◆ Write copy in brief, bouncy, down-to-earth style.

- ◆ Describe the product clearly and fully.

- ◆ Stress the "YOU" approach; tell how the offer will benefit the buyer.

- ◆ Avoid overtalking about yourself or your company.

- ◆ Strive for conviction and sincerity—be believable. Don't exaggerate.

- ◆ Stir the reader to action to order your product.

- ◆ Give specific, clear directions for ordering.

- ◆ Provide a guarantee of satisfaction or money back.

- ◆ Tailor the ad/literature to fit the prospect you want to reach.

> **CAUTION** It is unwise to offer money back guarantees on items priced very inexpensively, for example, a £3.00 report.

◆ Prepare the ad copy with care. It must fit your specific medium.

> **note**
> To evaluate your advertising cost, think in terms of cost per inquiry. This is calculated by dividing the number of inquiries into the cost of the ad. That cost may vary from about £0.50 to £1.30 or more.

◆ Don't make unreasonable claims, but remember that you are selling.

◆ Try to convince the reader that you are reliable and trustworthy.

◆ Key all ads to test their effectiveness.

◆ Always watch where your competitors are advertising.

◆ Experiment with new publications.

◆ It is generally considered impossible to sell something that costs more than £2.00 to £4.00 direct from either a classified ad or a small display ad. This is because there just is not enough space to convince someone to part with £10.00 or £20.00. It takes a full page ad to do that.

◆ Set up your own in-house advertising agency and save 15% on every ad you place.

Testing your offer

• If capital permits, test more than one magazine.

• Test more than one ad, each in a different publication.

• Try split runs if the magazine offers regional or sectional issues.

• Continue a successful ad without change until its pull drops to break-even point.

• Don't rush to change an ad that is pulling well; experiment slowly.

- Test only one change at a time: size of ad—copy—different appeal—new headline—another illustration—new price.

- Use short testimonials if space permits.

- Offer a bonus—something free or at reduced price.

- Key each ad or mailing to determine where results were derived from.

- Keep accurate records of returns from each promotion.

The advertising agency

The emphasis should be on YOU THE CUSTOMER, rather than I, the company.

- Select an advertising agency experienced in mail-order.

- Check their credentials; current accounts; successful promotions.

- Don't use agencies which represent direct competitors.

- Expect to pay in advance for ad placements and other services until credit terms are established.

- Advertising agencies are not infallible. Forgive an honest mistake. Give the agency at least a second chance.

- Expect to pay for preparation of display ads, copy layout, and other services you authorise. Classified ad copy will be prepared without any cost to you.

- Extend full cooperation; go along with their recommendations.

- If your advertising budget is substantial, consider setting up your own advertising agency—thereby saving 15% commission, plus a 2% discount in many instances.

Ad placement

- Newspapers with mail-order sections bring quick returns and are acceptable for initial test. Results are not usually as good as from magazine ads for long-range pull.

- Use only publications with the type of readership who will react favourably to your type of product or offer.

- Unsold inquirers should be followed up with special inducements or with new offers.

- Advertise in publications which feature large mail-order sections; place ads in the same issues or sections that your competitors advertise.

Sales literature

- Usually consists of sales letter, descriptive circular or folder, order form, return envelope (Some offers may be effectively sold by only a sales letter).

- Effective sales letter must create AIDA—Attention, Interest, Desire, Action.

- The circular should fully illustrate or describe the product. It must provide more detailed information about the product—its uses, benefits, advantages and other special appeals.

- Reply paid envelope is an essential part of sales literature to make it convenient for the customer to mail the order.

- Mailing sales offers by first-class mail vs. a mailsort option usually shows no appreciable difference in results.

- Mailing envelope can feature an attractive design or teaser message to induce the recipient to open and read the offer.

Responding to inquiries

- Each inquiry you receive in response to an ad should be answered via First-Class post, if at all possible, within 24 hours.

- The contents of the envelope going to the prospective customer should contain: a circular, promotional flier, or mini-brochure, a sales letter, an order form (the order form can be part of the circular), a return envelope, and other appropriate information, such as a fact sheet, a free report, etc.

- In general, circulars should be limited to one A4 sized page.

- A sales letter, on the other hand, can be as long as it takes to say everything you need to say to a prospective customer in order to sell him the product.

Postage and delivery

- Answer inquiries to your advertising immediately via First Class Post.

- You can save a great deal of money by investigating the various services currently on offer through the Royal Mail. For further details, ring the Sales Office on 0345 950950.

Watch your shipping weight. A fraction of an ounce can make a big difference in a large mailing.

- Keep your mailing lists clean—updated.

- Use all the various mail classes.

- Compare costs of carriers other than the Post Office.

- Guarantee return postage.

- Use plain but sturdy packaging to deliver orders.

- Send via Parcel Force or whichever alternative company is cheaper.

- Address labels with typewriter or computer; not by hand unless indelible ink is used and address printed.

- Specify "Return Guaranteed" on labels or package.

Printing cost

- Finding the right printing company takes time, so keep shopping until you find the right one.

- Very large printers will not be interested in your business. Very small ones, such as Pronto Print or Kall-Kwik, although convenient, are generally too expensive. Their equipment is not large enough to be competitive.

note Don't hesitate to use out of town printers. If you live in a high cost-of-living area, you can probably save a substantial amount of money. Many of these printers advertise in mail-order publications.

- There are many medium sized printers that will give you good pricing and quality printing. Often they have the capability to help you with layout and design.

- Use whatever promotional material is available from your supplier.

- Until you know what sells, print small quantities, even if it is more expensive.

- Use coloured paper for your promotional flyers to spice up your offer. Use white paper, blue or black ink for everything else.

Payments, refunds and complaints

- Accept cash, cheques and postal orders.

- ◆ Remember, the customer is always right. An argument won is usually a customer lost.

- ◆ If you receive an order with an underpayment, ship the order and invoice the customer for the difference.

- ◆ Make refunds on overpayments quickly.

- ◆ In order to comply with the industry's codes of practice (MOPS), most mail-order companies offer a 30-day money back guarantee. Some offer 90 days and even more.

- ◆ Avoid CODs unless you have collected enough to cover the costs of the return, plus costs of handling and repacking the merchandise.

- ◆ You need a special licence to offer credit terms, so don't offer to sell on credit or time payments until you have meet the legal requirements.

Record keeping

- • As in any business, it is important to keep records.

- • You need records to tell you what is going on in your business; to evaluate both your revenues and your expenses.

- • It is also required by law that you keep certain records.

- • Keep especially good records of your advertising expenses so you can evaluate your advertising on an ongoing basis.

Mailing lists

- ◆ Rent names only from reliable brokers or mail-order sources.

- ◆ Use only lists of people who are logical prospects for your offer.

- ◆ Offer your names to list brokers; this is a good source for extra income.

- ◆ Stay away from inexpensive mailing lists, under £25-£60 per 1,000.

- ◆ Avoid mailing lists whose owners make unrealistic claims.

- ◆ The best mailing list is your own list of buyers. Second best is your own list of inquirers.

Follow-up

- The most important factor in mail-order is FOLLOW-UP. Substantial profits can be generated from this segment, if it is properly handled.

- You can generate a lot of sales by including promotional material when filling orders for customers. Other orders are generated from mailings that are made to former customers, as well as individuals who inquired about an offer in the past.

- Send out regular mailings to your customers. At a minimum, four times per year. However, you can send out mailings as often as every 6 weeks or so, if you have a new product to offer.

- Send follow-up mailings of the same or similar offers to inquirers of advertising who did not buy the first time—2-4 additional mailings.

- As you build your mailing lists and you send out regular mailings, your orders will start flowing in.

Research and education

- ◆ Be on the lookout for new products you can offer your customers.

- ◆ Study the advertising of your competitors. Request their material and study it.

- ◆ Study all mailings you receive.

- ◆ If you are new to mail-order, read various publications that will improve your knowledge of the field.

The customer

- Consider the customer your greatest asset. Acknowledge that he is always right; even when he isn't.

- Handle complaints promptly; write courteous explanations.

- Offer replacement if product is broken or damaged.

An increasing number of mail-order companies accept credit cards—VISA and MasterCard for payment. It is generally felt that it does increase sales, especially if you take telephone orders.

note

- Issue immediate refunds; adjust overpayments promptly.

- Promote new or other products to your customer list. No other class of prospect will be as responsive.

- Work your customer list until it no longer proves profitable.

You

- You, mainly, control the destiny of your mail-order business.

- Be energetic; devote as much time as you can spare to advance your enterprise to a more profitable future.

- Be determined to make your mail-order business a huge success.

- Learn as much as you can about mail-order techniques.

- Be original; unique.

- Don't copy just anyone; copy only the successful methods and techniques; and always strive to improve on them.

- Keep searching diligently for new, "exclusive" products.

- Don't become disappointed by a slow start, or discouraged by a failure or two along the way.

- ◆ Always perform professionally; an amateur does not get paid for his services.

- ◆ Build your own financial pyramid; reinvest profits into productive programs that may mushroom your profits steadily.

- ◆ Avoid being an easy mark for "get-rich-quick" schemes; start and operate your business on sound principles.

Continue to learn about mail-order by reading, experimenting, and talking with other mail-order operators. Have patience. Success will not come overnight. It takes time to build a successful business. Start slowly and expand your business from your profits.

Best of luck!

note Whether you are new to this field or not, to stay on top, you must continue your education by reading books and reports on mail-order and subscribing to mail-order publications.

The biggest key to mail-order success

4

Chapter 4

The biggest key to mail-order success

What you'll find in this chapter:

- ⇒ Why you must specialise in a category
- ⇒ Why you must sell a line of related products
- ⇒ Why you must learn from others
- ⇒ The importance of "free offers"
- ⇒ Postage stamp marketing

Mail-order is a very complex business. Every phase must be planned, analysed and tested. The right demand products must be selected; the correct type of ads must be placed in the proper media and 1,001 other details must be attended to constantly.

A great number of people enter the mail-order field every week. What they find in many instances is that only three responses are received from 100 mailings, or that a £100 ad in a magazine with 4 million readers pulls 15 inquiries, and it appears hopeless. Especially after reading the glowing ads portraying the thousands that can be made overnight from your kitchen table! The mail-order enthusiast is led to believe that he should be able to hit it big immediately with little work. When he finds that this is not the case he drops out before he has a chance to learn, fearing that it will take too much of his television viewing time, or that it costs too much to get started on the road to profits! It does cost. Much more than the £10 or £20 often advertised as the total amount necessary to put £45,000 per year in their pocket!

Many continuously make fortunes in the mail-order business. However, if they can do it and you are one who thoroughly enjoys the world of mail-order, then there is no reason why you cannot make it also.

The biggest mistake in mail-order

> *note* Remember as you proceed on your way to ultimate success that there is no such thing as a failure—95% do not fail in the mail-order business—they just do not succeed!

Selling by mail is a goldmine, but not if you sell only one product

First, let's address the most frequent mistake that mail-order beginners make: failing to learn how the mathematics of mail-order work. It's simple. Consider all the expenses involved in selling your product: typesetting and printing your advertisement; buying (renting) the mailing list; and finally, postage. This is to name only the three main expenses.

Now, if you honestly think you're going to get rich by selling a £10 or £20 product to a few names, you are on the wrong path. You certainly could get rich selling a single product. It has happened countless times. Most probably you won't. Let's put it this way: your success would take several years. Anyway, that is not the way mail-order works.

The only way you can accelerate your growth and make money is if you sell a related line of products. Do not hesitate one moment: the people who make it big in mail-order are the ones that understand and apply this concept. The principle that lies behind this is that finding a customer is very expensive.

You sold something for £10 or £20 and then what? Do you forget about your new customer? No!! The true way to make money is to continue to supply that customer with additional related products.

There is no reason why you shouldn't do this. Sure, it's extra work. It is easier to make a sale, take the money and run. That's just too good to be true. Many folks still think that there are ways to make money the easy way, with no work at all, making

> **note** You have to work on your business everyday in order to become successful.

a million in one week and then spending the rest of their lives in the Caribbean.

Once you get a customer, it is so easy to get extra earnings from further sales that it's foolish not to offer him more products. You'd be letting go of the real bulk of your profit.

They must be related products. Here's why: If someone buys a book from you on "secret inexpensive advertising methods," it wouldn't be wise to then send him/her an advertisement on computer software. That person is now more likely to be interested in buying a report on "the biggest mistakes to avoid" or looking for renting a name list to mail out his recently published booklet. Get the picture? This is the idea of a Product Line. You don't need to offer expensive items and expensive sales brochures to follow this procedure successfully. Prepare an informative set of circulars of reports, or books, on a certain general subject like, for example, the ever popular "making money in mail-order," which is a safe subject to get into (most people are interested in making money from their homes).

The only way the small mail-order operator can find the way to big earnings is to specialise in a certain area. Your sales literature should offer products from a certain category, and mailed to a specifically targeted group of people. Therefore, you are minimising expenses and increasing the probabilities of making more sales per piece mailed.

> **note** Mail-order is a hot business, not only for big companies but also for the little guy who starts from his kitchen table.

Think about this: If you mail 1000 envelopes to a list of names you just rented, it costs you exactly the same money, as if you send out a circular offering a book than if you send along 4-5 circulars offering related reports, or books, etc. OK, you spent some extra money on printing those other circulars, but you spent the same on postage and on the names lists. If your potential customer is not interested in that single item you offered, you just threw away all that money. However, if you mailed out 4, 5 or 10 different offers you have a much better chance of pulling one or more orders.

In conclusion: the odds of making money are against you. They will be in your favour only when you have more than one product to offer, or better yet, 4, 5 or more. Specialise in one particular field. Target to that specific market through specialised publications or mailing lists. Conduct a decent business in order to keep people satisfied and needing to buy more products from you. If you put all this small extra effort in, you will be rewarded with a profitable share of this mail-order market.

Marketing is the key to mail-order success

Do you really know what marketing is? It's the art of finding ways to sell a product or service. But developing new ways of selling a product are not easy. You have to study what other people are doing and get ideas from them.

Get your mind in a direction to sell your product. Of course it helps if you created your own product or wholeheartedly believe in the product you are selling.

Tip

Listen to people who actually have something to show for their efforts. They know because they were there! Why seek marketing advice from a book that reads above your head and was only written by someone who studied the field? Go and talk to the people who actually lived it! There is a difference!

Now, all you have to do is find the type of people that are interested in buying your product. Find out what makes people buy a product like yours. Study how others are selling a similar product.

Then, armed with all this valuable information, work out a direct plan that you'll enjoy doing. Design methods around your likes, dislikes and personality traits. It works!

You also have to treat customers like you would your own family—with respect and concern. This does not mean you are to be shallow and allow yourself to be taken advantage of.

Even if you work outside the home 8 hours a day, you have to devote some time each evening to your home business enterprise.

Most businesses that last have seen hundreds or even thousands of new businesses open and close. That's one reason why people are sceptical of a new business until they see for themselves that they're serious. You have to prove that you are serious in order to get people to order from you and become good customers.

Customer service is nothing more than placing yourself in the other person's shoes and seeing the world and the situation from their viewpoint. Often, if you just take a few minutes to listen to people, you will learn a lot and turn a complaint into a workable situation.

In marketing, it is extremely important to start watching people and their buying habits. The next time you are standing at the checkout counter buying groceries—watch people around you. Don't stare at them, but open up your eyes and ears. Be in touch with your surroundings. Listen to ladies as they discuss the reason why they would rather buy one type of breakfast cereal over another brand name. Try and pick apart the actual reason why people react the way they do.

Here are some tips to help you appear professional and serious to potential customers in your mail-order business:

- On your word processor or computer, type a standard letter about your company. It should say something like: *"We would like to introduce our company to you. We are business professionals who are interested in providing our customers with the very best service available. We'll do our utmost to guarantee your satisfaction and repeat business. Enclosed are some offers for your consideration. They were specially selected for you and your interests. If you don't see what you're looking for—please take the time to write and let us know what we can do for you. We'd love to hear from you today."*

- Keep a list of all the mail-order publishers you come across. Then, if you ever move or introduce a new product to the market, you could send them a short press release. This works! Publishers are always looking for news to pass along to their readers.

- Give something away free for every order placed (depending on the amount of the order.) You might even want to give the customer a choice of the free items he/she can obtain for every order over £10, £25, £50 and £100. Instead of 50% off, offer to double the order. (For instance, instead of 50% off an order of 250 printed circulars—say that you'll double the order to 500 free.)

How to avoid the smaller, more common mail-order mistakes

Not everyone has worked in an office atmosphere all his or her life. When this type of person decides to go into mail-order business, they are not used to communicating with other dealers and potential customers. This lack of communication can close a mail-order business faster than lightning.

Here are some tips to make your transition smoother:

1) **Use a business sized envelope** (not the short ones you use to write to your mother) that contains the full name and address of the person you are writing to.

2) **Include a note or a letter**

Nothing is more frustrating than receiving an order from a customer with a cheque or cash enclosed with no explanation of what the person is ordering. Beginners often forget that the average mail-order dealer has hundreds or even thousands of products and services on offer. Many of those items might be priced the same. An example of a good cover letter would be:

Dear (name)

I noticed your advertisement in (name of publication) and would like to order your (name of product you are ordering). Thank you for your attention to this matter.

(Your name and address)

You can write this information on a post-it note and attach it to your cheque. However, it is more professional to use a standard sheet of A4 paper and put your name and address at the top of the sheet. This way the dealer can clearly read your name and address and fill your order. In your covering letter you might want to mention that you are new to mail-order and appreciate any information to help you out. Often, dealers extend a helpful hand to others.

3) **Don't expect your order in two days.**

Some people see an advertisement, order an item on Monday and expect to receive it by Thursday of the same week. That is impossible. Try to rationalise that it takes two – three days to receive first and second class post. Then it takes another three to ten days for most dealers to fill their orders. Most beginners don't realise that there are some mail-order people processing an average of 200 – 1,000 pieces of post each day. It's hard to imagine.

Most don't have employees to help, so try and have a little patience and understanding when placing an order. If you place an order with a national mail-order house, don't they advise you to allow 4-6 weeks for your order to arrive? Give small dealers the same courtesy.

4)   Be specific.

Would you send BT or your gas company a cheque for £50 and expect them to know what account you were making a payment on? Of course you wouldn't – so how are mail-order businesses supposed to know what you're ordering or requesting? Sending a note saying "Send me info" will not tell a business what you are ordering. Most mail-order businesses carry a large number of different products. If they send you information on everything they sell, not only would it cost a lot more in postage and heavy duty envelopes, but you'll also get a lot of different information on products you may not be interested in. In fact, the business may not include the information you originally requested because they had no idea what you ordered and couldn't afford to send you everything they have.

note Not everyone can provide 24 hour service, especially if the mail-order business owner is very busy. Some have personal lives that take up time – they don't spend every waking moment processing orders.

Okay. Let's be realistic. If you are guilty of inflicting pain on dealers by not letting them know what you are ordering or requesting information for, don't worry. They don't hate you and want you to slink away in shame. On the contrary, they want your business and they want to keep you happy as a steady customer.

A correct form of writing a business letter should go something like this:

Dear (Name):

We noticed your advertisement in (name of publication) and would like more information on (product or service). Your attention to this matter is greatly appreciated.

If you don't want to take the time to write this much, you could just cut out the ad you saw and tape it on your letterhead or note paper. Enclose the proper stamps, money or SAE for a reply and you're ready to send it off.

TIP The next time you order something, read your note or letter one time before putting it in the envelope and sealing it shut. Ask yourself if you have provided enough information to process your order. That's all there is to it!

Mail-order laws and regulations

5

Chapter 5

Mail-order laws and regulations

This chapter provides an overview of those laws and regulations that most affect the small mail-order operator. The intent is not to give legal advice. Such advice should always be sought from a solicitor. Only those laws and regulations that most directly apply to the small order operator are covered. Advice is given from the perspective of an operator of a mail-order business rather than from a legal perspective.

note For those interested in an in-depth review of the laws which affect the mail-order and direct mailing industries, it is recommended that you contact the Office of Fair Trading, who publish information on all of these matters.

The voluntary codes of practice

As a beginner to the mail-order business, the first "law" that you'll come into contact with isn't really a law at all, but a voluntary code of practice used by just about every newspaper and periodical in the country. Basically, this code of practice controls the quality of service and the nature of the products contained in the advertisements appearing in their publications. The codes are designed to ensure that consumers are given the highest degree of protection from cowboy traders– so it is in your best interest to learn more about them.

The British Codes of Advertising and Promotions have developed through the years. New rules are incorporated as they come along. While there is no legal obligation for traders to follow the provisions of these codes of practice, they are, in effect, the backbone of the self-regulatory process in the UK and as administered by the Advertising Standards Authority (ASA) will continue to affect how you operate your business. You will quickly learn that although there are different version of this code, they all cover the same basic territory.

In order to maintain their readers' trust, newspapers and magazines have willingly implemented the guidelines laid out by the ASA. These publications accept the responsibility of making sure that the ads they run (and the offers behind them) are legal, decent, honest and true. In other words, they take it upon themselves to guarantee that you and your product are what you say they are.

The quickest and easiest way to familiarise yourself with these requirements is to obtain details of the Mail Order Protection Scheme (MOPS) from their office on 020 7269 0520. Alternatively, you could obtain the much more detailed publication about the codes of practice from the main office of The British Code of Advertising Practice or Sales Promotion Practice, on 020 7580 5555.

For the purposes of getting you started, I'll list the most important requirements.

1. If you are asking for money in advance, your full name and trading address must be included in your ad. A PO box number and postcode does not constitute a full address. In fact, many publications will not allow you to use a PO box number at all – so ask, if you are unsure about this.

> **note** Many of the points covered might not affect your business at first, but as you expand and develop your marketing and advertising techniques, it will put you ahead of the game to know precisely how to use these regulations to your own benefit.

2. If you are following a two stage selling option, whereby a free catalogue or list is being advertised, then you may use a PO box number, but only if you provide your full name and address in the reply you send back to the inquirer.

3. The description of your product must be true and accurate – this means in both the verbal and implied descriptions, i.e. the illustrations. You may, of course, be enthusiastic and describe your product in glowing terms, but not beyond the bounds of reality.

4. Your price claims must be authentic. You should, for instance, check with the Office of Fair Trading on any legal position for your type of product. Be aware that words such as "free", "new" and "sale" carry strict interpretations with them. Free must mean exactly that, and new should only be used when new items are actually used. A "sale" is a reduction from the seller's own former price of a given article. The seller must have sold, not just offered the article, for a reasonable period of time. This simply means that if a 50% discount is offered on a £10.00 book, the book at some previous time must have actually been sold at £10.00. If it just has a cover price of £10, but was always sold at £7.00, a £5.00 price is not a 50% discount.

5.   Your product must be safe, of a satisfactory quality, and fit for the purpose for which it is sold.

6.   If you use testimonials in your ads, you must be prepared to give proof of the customers' existence. You'll need written authorisation to use their comments, which is signed, dated and contains a contact address, in case the publications ask to see them.

The Mail Order Protection Scheme, mentioned earlier, specifically covers the supply and shipping of your products. If you have agreed to abide by the newspapers' or periodicals' particular code of practice, you will be bound to do the following for your customers:

- You must ship your customers' orders within a reasonable amount of time. This is commonly understood to be within 28 days from the time the order and payment are received. If you are unable to do so, then you must tell your customer. If the customer has paid in advance, you must offer him a refund, but if he declines this refund, preferring to wait until you can fill the order, then you must provide him with a firm date of despatch or a fortnightly progress report.

- You must allow your customer to return their order to you if the product proves unsatisfactory, and you must allow them a minimum of seven days in which to do so.

- If you are unable to fill an order or a special promotional offer for reasons outside your control, then a product of similar or greater value must be substituted.

- You must provide your customer with a full refund when their order is returned, or if the order never reaches them (lost in the post on the outward journey). Additionally, you must issue a refund if they claim they've returned the product to you and have proof of posting, even though the product never reached you (lost in post on the return journey).

- You may not send unsolicited goods and then demand payment.

- If you send free samples, they must be clearly identified as such, and you cannot have charged the recipient post and packing for them.

Prizes and promotions

If you're thinking about offering promotions with prize draws or competitions, you should first familiarise yourself with the Lotteries and Amusements Act 1976, which governs such activities quite specifically. You can obtain a copy of this Act from a Stationery Office (formerly the HMSO) in your local area. This type of activity is not going to be for the initiates into the mail-order business, but rather for those who are taking their business to a whole new level of operation. For the ambitious then, be aware of the following points:

1. Prize draws must be free. The chance of winning the prize draw must be equal for everyone exposed to your competition, whether they have actually purchased your goods or not. No special skills are required to win, and no entry price – in any shape or form – can be charged.

2. Competitions or contests, on the other hand, are prize schemes where the prize is awarded on the basis of merit rather than chance. You must therefore award the prizes on the basis of skill and judgement. You must establish a judging panel and make the rules of entry available to all entrants. You are allowed, however, to decide just whom the entrants will be; they may well have to be actual paying customers.

3. Games in this case are either games of chance or competitions, and will be treated in law as lotteries or competitions, according to their precise nature. Beware! The laws surrounding lotteries can be very complex, so before you make the decision to offer a game, consult a specialist first.

Data Protection Act 1998

DEFINITION

This law will directly affect you if you decide to store your lists of names and addresses on a computerised system. The law was designed to safeguard the public from abuse in the collection, storage and distribution of personal information. It gives consumers the right to object to their details being held in such a manner, and you as the supplier must give them the chance to inform you of their decision.

Once you have chosen to computerise your lists, you must immediately register with the Data Protection Registrar, on 01625 545 745. They will provide you with the most up to date guidance notes to help you meet your obligations. Here's a list of the types of information you will need to give them in order to complete the registration process:

- Your full name and address

- A description of how you plan to use the data you've collected

- What type of data and where you have obtained the data

- An indication of any other parties with whom you intend to share, swap or sell such information

- A list of any countries outside the UK to which this information might be transferred

Once this has been done, and provided you give your customers a clear and repeated chance to indicate their wishes on the matter, you should have no trouble with the law.

Law concerning the direct marketing industry

There is a Direct Marketing Code of Practice as well, an industry code which works in practice with current legislation and the British Codes of Advertising Practice. Members of the Direct Marketing Association undertake to adhere to the code and accept that if they break the terms of the code, the result may well be a disciplinary proceeding.

The code applies to all the links in the Direct Marketing chain, from advertisers to mailing houses, list brokers and managers to database bureaux, with a particular emphasis on the rules relating to list and database users. If you feel that Direct Mail is the best way forward, I highly recommend that you contact the Direct Marketing Association for a copy of their code, priced at £10.00, on 020 7321 2525.

What is copyright?

DEFINITION

Copyright is the right given by statutes to the creators of original works of a literary, dramatic, musical or artistic nature to prevent others from copying, publishing, performing or otherwise exploiting their works without permission. It arises automatically when the work is created, so there is no registration procedure - no forms to fill in and no fees to pay. It lasts for the lifetime of the creator, plus a further 70 years, so just because something was first produced a long time ago, it doesn't mean that it is safe for you, or anyone else, to copy it.

Copyright may exist in text, design, sound recordings, forms and any similar material, which would not necessarily be thought "artistic". For instance, an entry form for the football pools has been held to be protected. However, copyright does not protect ideas. It may protect a work that expresses an idea, but not the idea behind it.

Although the first copyright automatically belongs to the author, he may pass it on to others by licence (as with a publisher who may, for instance, publish books but not make films) or by outright assignment. If you have employees whose job includes the creation of original material, you should get them to sign an assignment to you of future copyright in any work they produce in the course of their employment.

If you have any further questions on the matter, don't hesitate to get in touch with The Patent Office. You can contact them either by telephone or in writing, although many of your questions could be answered by a visit to their website: www.patent.gov.uk.

Postal laws

Law prohibits some things from being sent through the post. The despatch of such items could harm either Royal Mail staff or the recipient, so if they are discovered, they will either be returned to you or they will be disposed of without prior notice. In the worst case scenario, Royal Mail will bring a claim against you, so to avoid all threat of prosecution, stay well away from the following products:

aerosols, butane lighters, counterfeit currency, bank notes and postage stamps (unless copies of obsolete items), drugs prohibited for general use by law, flammable liquids or solids, indecent, obscene or offensive material, living creatures, matches, paints, varnishes, enamels and similar substances, and sharp items.

For full details on the dos and don'ts of postal use, contact your local Post Office counter, or visit them on their website at: www.royalmail.co.uk.

How to start your own company

Once you decide that you want to go into business, you must set yourself up to get started. There are generally three ways to structure a business entity: The sole proprietorship, where you run the business on your own, the partnership, where you run it with other people, and the corporation, which is run by a company properly formed at Companies House with shareholders and directors.

If you choose one of the first two options, your business will be unincorporated and if you choose the third, your business will be incorporated. There are advantages and disadvantages to any of these options that will depend greatly on your own particular circumstances. Therefore, you must take the time to learn which one will best suit your needs. Always seek professional advice before committing yourself.

note

After deciding upon this basic question, you must then give serious attention to the name of your business. There are particular rules about company names, so again, a bit of research into the matter is highly recommended. For instance, the name you choose must not suggest a connection with royalty.

Other names might have been previously registered at the Trade Marks Registry, so you must check with that office to make sure no one can object to the name you are choosing for your business. Finally, you should be aware of names that confuse the public into thinking that they are dealing with a different, perhaps a better known or well-established company than yourself. You could be accused of "passing off" by this other company, so proceed carefully.

How to sell information by mail

Chapter 6

How to sell information by mail

What you'll find in this chapter:

- ▶ Who buys information
- ▶ Writing and preparing the manuscript
- ▶ Copyrighting your material
- ▶ Manuscripts on cassette
- ▶ The best books to sell by mail
- ▶ How to reach the hobby and collectors' markets

How to sell your own written material

Selling information by mail is surely one of the most profitable business operations today. You can start a small business for yourself and make it flourish.

You don't have to be a writer or have experience in running a business. All the steps in setting up a mail-order business are simple, easy to follow, and may reap a steady second income for you - even building up to a highly profitable full-time enterprise.

You don't need to give up anything. All the tips given in the following pages require minimum expense, can be done at home, and need only a small but constant amount of your time.

note The advantages of your own business are endless, but most of all, you have a feeling of accomplishment and fulfilment, as you help other people acquire the knowledge they want – and will pay for.

What you do need is the desire to make it work. If you have perseverance to follow through, and the discipline to complete each of the steps, then you are well on your way to creating something special for yourself.

Why sell information?

Bookshops mostly cater to mass market books and paperbacks; record shops carry only popular recording artists. Where can you get information on a specific topic? Even specialised magazines are limited in their scope and the information they cover.

You can order items by mail in the safety and privacy of your own home. You don't have to shop around at the shops, wasting time and petrol. You have a direct connection with the seller of the information, often being able to write specific questions and get feedback-especially with newsletters and courses.

Mail-order at home provides a high profit margin. Producing written or recorded information is inexpensive compared to the price you can receive. You can operate with a low overhead, the business is simple to run, and there is no middle seller. Cheques come directly to you.

note People achieve success because they know something special. Specialised knowledge and "how to" are the most sought after types of information successfully sold by mail-order.

What can I sell?

There is an endless need for specialised information that you probably have on hand, or can easily obtain. You don't have to be an expert to produce and sell that information.

Specialised information may be anything from a favourite set of recipes to a list of the fastest horse tracks in the country. It can include places to visit, such as back roads, country inns or fine restaurants in an area. It can be reliable sources for special goods, and titbits of information about a special subject.

"How to" can be anything from making Christmas decorations to finding a good place for camping and hiking. It can be plans, instructions or tips on how to make something, or find a special place, or achieve a special goal. It may pertain to sports, hobbies and self-improvement. Or, it may relate directly to the hundreds of speciality publications such as skiing, decorating or writing songs.

You have imagination

Information is not limited to books and cassettes. It comes in many forms. Something you may sell for a little money and only a few pages might be plans or directions. A short piece (up to 50 pages) may be a report, manual, folio or pamphlet.

Later, if you get into multiple printing, photo illustrations, and many items to offer, you might produce brochures, catalogues booklets or directories.

Think about what you might have to offer, and how much commitment you want to make. Maybe

> **TIP**
>
> If you're really good at what you do, you might even start a newsletter or correspondence course, both of which can earn a great deal of money and provide ongoing income for years.

you want to prepare a short report, make a few photocopies and test the results. Or, maybe you are prepared for a larger project such as a book or a series of cassettes.

You know something special

Because your life is unique, you have knowledge and experience that is helpful to others. You have encountered and accomplished thousands of tasks that you have taught to friends, children or work associates. What's sometimes hard for another person might be easy for you, and that's why you loaned a helping hand.

note

It is this information, this specialised knowledge that sells at a large profit.

TIP
Stuck for an idea? You can generate your own ideas. Think about what you could write about as you go through your day. You know something special at work. You may cook a delicious recipe. You may know how to fix things easily.

What do you have a special interest in? You probably do several unusual things well. Do you know how to make something that relatives think is great? Have you read about a specific subject for years as a pet interest? Maybe there's something that you would like to look into, find out about, and share-something that other people are looking into too.

Look through magazine racks and bookshops for ideas. There's always something you always wanted to know about. Try the library and the Yellow Pages for sources. Talk to your family and friends. Encourage yourself.

Who will buy?

 Take a look in the classified ads section of your favourite magazines and tabloids. What kind of information is offered? Watch the repeats. Ads which offer the same materials month after month are winners.

You can be a winner too. You can easily produce and sell information in the form of short reports or longer booklets and make the same profit as these others.

Take a look at the price. Invest a little and write away for some of the materials similar to what you want to do. What do you like? What would you avoid?

Analyse your potential customer. What does that person expect? The same as you. You are a perfect example of your own customer. And, although you're willing to pay for special information that's inexpensive to reproduce, you expect your money's worth. That's what makes repeat business and turns potential into real money.

You have something to say

Your enthusiasm will show. The amount of pleasure you get from the topic will come through the pages of the report. Go ahead - be creative. But, get the facts straight. Write what you know about. It must be original and unique. You should have something different to offer, something important to say, especially if you write about a well-known subject.

Preparing a manuscript is easy

After you have chosen a topic and decided on the approximate length, now what? You don't need to become a world authority on your subject, but research it.

Read several booklets or reports similar in format and subject matter. Compare the type of information and the depth of research. You might want to subscribe to the magazines

> note
>
> You can write. Don't be afraid – there's no one marking your efforts. You have the ability to put ideas down on paper in a logical sequence that makes sense to other people. That's it. It's that easy.

pertaining to the topic (you may already). And, of course, talk to others that can give you input.

Keep moving. You can begin writing as you research so you don't get caught in the bog of details. Prepare a basic outline or a list of the points you wish to cover, and write them out.

Can somebody help?

At any stage of the writing process you can hire somebody to help. A "ghost-writer" can prepare manuscript from your idea and outline. An editor can polish even the roughest copy into full, complete prose. Even a good typist can take rough copy, punctuate it, and make it more readable.

All of these people can be found by placing a small ad in the newspaper or from the classifieds in writers' magazines. You'd be surprised it doesn't cost that much and you won't have to agonise over the manuscript.

Tips on writing

If you can write a letter, you can write a short report. In fact, that's the best attitude-as though you're writing to a friend. Because what you offer is basically sound, friendly advice or instructions in the form of information.

The best writing is clear, easy to read, and follows an understandable sequence. Be careful not to meander or repeat. Each idea or separate point should have a beginning, middle, and an end.

Be careful to always assume the basic intelligence of your reader – don't talk down. Although you are giving someone new information, that person may – and usually does – know a great deal about the subject.

Use subheads to break up the blocks of writing and write short paragraphs and simple sentences. This is not a contest for best prose, but be sure to use the basic rules of grammar and punctuation.

Be sure to include helpful information, tips, or any keys to reading illustrations. Again, you don't have to be an artist to draw a simple stick figure picture, as long as it's clear and explains what you want to convey.

The standard manuscript form is typed, double space with side and top margins of about 1 1/2 inches and at least a one-inch margin at the bottom. If you are not an expert typist or don't have an excellent quality typewriter, hire someone to complete the finished copy. It's not expensive and is absolutely necessary, since that is your product.

You must have something to say. Reread your manuscript and scrutinise it to be sure you have something valuable to offer. That's a basic key to success in selling information.

Go slowly at first

 You have your manuscript and you're ready for printing. Don't go to the expense of professional volume printing - not yet. Investigate your local instant press printers. Photo offset is a very inexpensive and efficient way to reproduce copies from several hundred to several thousand.

If you want to test a few dozen at first, even photocopies are reasonable in price. Since you have a clean manuscript, the copies will be clear and easy to read - a product to be proud of.

What about cassettes?

Pre-recorded cassettes are an excellent way to sell information by mail. There's a large profit in these too! Drivers listen to cassettes while commuting and sales managers use them to follow up on seminars and meetings. With all the sound equipment available and in use today, recorded information is in great demand.

You'd be surprised how inexpensive it is to record and mass duplicate cassettes for your business of selling information. First, have a prepared manuscript to read from, and you get someone with a pleasant speaking voice to do the actual recording.

Because you need only the speaking quality recording tape, you can purchase cassettes in quantity at a very low price. Cassettes are available from bulk loading companies in any length to match the exact minutes of recorded information. That way there's no blank tape at the end, which is amateur and wastes money.

You can use a good tape recorder at home to record your information. It should have a clear, excellent sound, with no static or interference. Of course, be sure to eliminate background noises that detract from the recording. Remember, this is a business, and your product must be high quality. Later, when the orders roll in, you can go into a recording studio to produce the finest quality recording.

Like printed matter, cassettes are easily mailed. Purchase cases to go with the cassettes that are being sent out. Later, you can even have cassette insert cards printed up to achieve a fine looking product.

High-speed duplicating services will mass-produce tapes for you at a very reasonable price. Investigate quality and compare costs before you commit yourself.

How to protect yourself

To protect your rights against anyone else using what you publish, copyright the material. Both printed and recorded materials can be copyrighted. Copyright protection in the UK is automatic. Don't worry about unpublished manuscripts - they are protected against unauthorised copying. But, as soon as you send information to the public, it is in the public domain unless it carries a copyright notice.

The notice may appear in one of three forms: the word "copyright", "copr." or the symbol "©". It must appear on the title page or the page immediately following the title page and include the name of the owner and the year it was published.

For further information, don't hesitate to contact The Patent Office, either through their website: www.patent.gov.uk, or at the following address: The Patent Office, Harmsworth House, 13 –15 Bouverie Street, London EC4Y 8DP, telephone number for the Central Enquiry Unit: 0645 500 505.

How to sell books by mail

Now that you've written that attractive report, how are you going to sell it? Perhaps you have already tried by placing a carefully written classified or maybe a large display ad, then waited for the postman to pile the flood of orders in your box. What happened? The odds are 100 to 1 that you came up with a couple of orders for all the time and effort. Why? You see continuous ads, small ones and full-page £4,000 ads in newspapers, and magazines offering books and information. Many of them are repeated over and over again by the same advertiser. You know that they are making it or they could not continue to advertise month after month. How are they making it when you don't seem to have any luck?

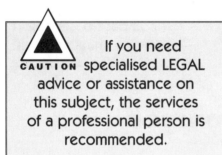

If you need specialised LEGAL advice or assistance on this subject, the services of a professional person is recommended.

By examining the operations of these successful people we find that they use several simple and easy methods to produce excessive profits in the mail-order book selling business. When you know these methods and put them to work you will find that you have the opportunity to make big money in this business.

To start yourself on the road to success by writing your own books or reports and then selling them...Anytime and every time you think of an idea or book title, write it down immediately. Regardless of how idiotic it may appear to you at first, it could be the ingredient you need to start you on the way to a fortune. File your notes and look them over periodically. You put yourself in a position where you have a good chance to come up with an idea or a title that will be a real moneymaking blockbuster.

If your writings are about your own experiences on an inspirational or how-to subject, consider writing the book as well as the ads that sell it, in the "first person". This gives the reader the feeling he is getting personal communication and is not just a number in a computer.

note When tests indicate you have a winner, all that is left to do is expand the advertising in the proper media and fill orders.

Many in mail-order business have indicated that it is not a good policy and often a waste of time and money to advertise in a general daily or weekly newspaper. This is true under ordinary circumstances, but we find that when you have a particularly "strong" title it pays to place conservative "test" ads in the newspaper in order to learn the results quickly. However, one must keep extensive records in order to compare results and determine if they may have a winner.

It is advisable to structure the price of your book so an offer will stand an advertising expense of at least one-half of the selling price. You need to spend this much for advertising in order to be successful.

note A 100% guarantee is a must in the book selling business. Not everyone who purchases your book, regardless of how great it is, is going to benefit from it. There are always a few who will want their money back. Have a unique guarantee, which reassures them they haven't spent their money until they are satisfied.

For the author/self-publisher, selling by mail is really the only way to go. The production costs are low because the value is in the information, not necessarily in the number of pages written. Mail-order is one of the finest businesses ever for the little guy who wants the opportunity to try for serious money. All you have to do is test with just small expenditure, correct your mistakes and let the business expand itself!

note Action pictures used in your ads get fabulous results if handled right. Especially productive are ideas showing your product in action.

If you are able to write a self improvement book or handbook with very valuable information and at the same time make it lively, witty and interesting, you could have the makings of a bankable winner. After your first tests prove reasonable; determine if a more reasonable price structure will produce better net profit through appealing to a large audience. When you find it hitting, promote it in every way possible. Send out several hundred copies to book reviewers to get write-ups in as many publications as possible. Learn to deal with the many small booksellers and bookshops, or cooperate with some large distributors to get the books out through their normal channels.

Search out the drawings and pictures used in better ads that run month after month to learn what effective copywriting is all about, then use the same ideas for your comparative publication.

When you find the right combination (title, body and ad), a lot of money can be made in a short time and it is a great thrill to write an ad, test it, and see the money pouring in from your own creative ability.

Publish your book yourself, and you also control the entire operation. If it doesn't sell, you must abandon it before the heavy promotional expenditures bury you. You remain flexible and diversified when you are your own publisher.

Run some small classified advertisements in *The Times* or, if in London, *The Evening Standard*, as well as other good publications to get inquiries. When enough books are sold to more than cover the cost of the ads and mailings, slowly, as the profits build, run more and larger ads. As sales prove your publications to be winners, you can run full-page ads in national magazines, inviting direct orders with a coupon included in the ads.

The large publishing companies use a shotgun approach, publishing many titles while profiting from the few successful ones. They can't begin to market effectively all the many books on their list. Trying to sell your book through them is generally futile.

Remember, as you sit down to write, the information should be about something in which you are knowledgeable and interested, or something you thoroughly researched. It must have some value for the readers and they should benefit by having read it. If it is not helpful to the reader and the benefits are not there, sales cannot be sustained.

In summary, your book must fill a genuine need; the price structure must be correct, there has to be a large or mass market for the information in your book, your advertising must be believable and offer a strong guarantee, and you must thoroughly test before investing substantial amounts to promote and sell the book.

How to make it in the mail-order wholesale book business

The real profit in selling books by mail comes from having dealers sell for you. Rather than mailing thousands of your own mailing packets, at today's high postage, get thousands mailed through your own dealers. This can generate steady orders and profits and is one of the secrets to a successful mail-order book business.

There are a number of mail-order firms offering good mail-order distributorships. They offer quality books, reports and folios that appeal to the public; the kind of publications that consistently generate high profits in the mail-order business.

note You should give wholesale book selling a try. Recognise the profit potential and determine if this method fits in with you other programmes.

Most of the better firms offering distributorships have a simplified programme which includes instructions, profit tested literature, sales letters, brochures, order forms and return envelopes that do the selling job for you. These simple

> **TIP** You should make every effort to purchase publications for a minimum of four time below retail price. In other words, you purchase 100 booklets for £1 each = £100; you sell to your dealers at £2 each = £200; your dealer must realise at least double his cost when selling to the consumer, or £4 = £400.

instructions can be followed even by the inexperienced person. The old timers in mail-order can use the wholesale book selling programs to supplement their other projects, in many instances combining book selling with their other mailing activities with very little added expense.

Imprinted sales literature, to solicit dealers and for the dealers to use in selling to the consumer, is furnished at reasonable prices; or camera ready copy is usually available so that the printing can be done locally. The literature for dealers is priced a little higher than cost to pay for processing the order.

The source will ship your customers' orders for literature, brochures, etc., under your shipping label. They will also drop-ship the books and publications direct to your dealers, using your name or label.

Your wholesale cost for publications will vary depending on whether you have the Prime Source drop-ship direct to your dealers, or in quantity to your place of business. The amount you charge your dealers will also vary depending on drop-ship services or quantify purchases.

You must ascertain that the Prime Source carries sufficient inventory with a number of different titles and that titles may be assorted in making up quantity when you purchase in volume. Determine if shipments are made promptly and if the Prime Source pays all handling and shipping charges so that your cost is "Net". Even though your cost is "Net", you must pay for shipping to your dealers; they must absorb the cost of mailing to their customers.

The price you have to pay the Prime Source often is the determining factor in the success of your program. If the book retails at a price too low, considering the high postage and mailing costs, no profit can be realised by your dealer, nor by yourself, unless orders are limited to a minimum number of titles for each total purchase. Be certain that the program offered by the Prime Source allows sufficient margin to pay for all your costs, and your dealers, while generating a fair profit for you both.

To find the right programs for your operation, write to a number of firms offering book selling wholesale programs. These can be found in any of the hundreds of mail-order adsheets, magazines and publications available today.

Get their literature, then order a minimum starting packet of the programs that interest you and fit in with your mail-order business schedule. Make tests to prove the value of each program. Drop those that do not prove out after a reasonable test. When you find one that is hitting, multiply it cautiously until you know it is a winner, then go full blast in every direction to make it pay off BIG!

The best books to sell by mail

Best books to sell by mail? First, forget about fiction! These can be purchased from any high street bookshop, found at the library, or bought through the large mail-order book clubs. Scientific, technical, and textbooks are other categories to stay away from. All others have good mail-order potential. There is a broad market on religious books, especially those dealing with "End Times". However, the various church outlets control most books in this classification.

Mystic and metaphysical books are more or less a specialised field and generally the demand is not large. Health and recreation books have a steady market, but they are mostly tied up by firms in the catalogue business. Self help and do-it-yourself books are best for newcomers.

To start in the book selling business, first get sample books of the ones you think you would like to sell. Get mailing lists of book buyers and opportunity seekers; start advertising for inquiries rather than first trying to sell the books direct through the mail.

Choose the type of books that interest you the most. You can better enjoy and promote things you like. Keep card records for each of your customers. Above all guarantee satisfaction and back it up with prompt and courteous refund policies.

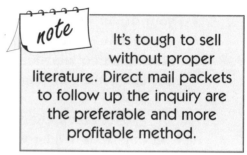

note It's tough to sell without proper literature. Direct mail packets to follow up the inquiry are the preferable and more profitable method.

How to sell short reports

Several dealers give you permission to reproduce their various short reports and sales letters. You will often find some of these reports sell equally well direct to the consumer, beginners in mail-order, and to the seasoned dealers.

Here are a few ways to make the most money with them:

1) Have circulars printed, listing the reports by title, selling them for £1 each, or say 5 for £3. Include a circular in all outgoing packages and letters.

2) Place small ads in mail-order trade magazines similar to the following:
    Why pay when you can get it free? Sources of Free Mailing Lists £1.00; Sources of Free Commission Circulars £1.00; How to get Cirx. Mailed Free £1.00 [your name and address here].

3) Reproduce sales letters that sell your reports, including reproduction rights, inserting your name as the Prime Source. Mail this sales letter to your own list or one that you purchase.

4) Place small classified ads in national mail-order magazines and send the sales letters to the inquiries. A good ad for this purpose follows:
    2000% Profit, selling information by mail.
    Free report tells how. Send SAE [your name and address].

5) Some of these reports sell quite well from small classified and space ads. The best way to use this method is to offer a single report for £1.00 then fill the order with the report plus the sales letter which offers all of the reports and reproduction rights. Here is a typical classified ad:
    HOW TO make £100 a day. Complete instructions! £1.00.

In addition to giving you a small profit, these reports are designed to build up your mailing list. Generally speaking, because the reports are so cheap to produce, you can offer them free just to get fresh names in exchange. There is no need to have a large quantity of them printed up until you develop a feel for the best sellers for your operation.

The firms who initially sell you these products usually offer to print the reports and letters for a fee. For those who don't want to stock the reports, they generally drop-ship direct to your customer for 50% upon receipt of an address label and information on what reports to ship.

How to get and sell name lists

There are numerous methods of obtaining and selling name lists. If you want to prepare a national directory of mail-order operators, how do you get the listings? One way is to advertise that you are creating such a directory and will list them therein upon receiving their name and address, together with a brief description of their operations and activity.

note Many list brokers across the country have lists available for rent or sale. The lists cover every imaginable classification of potential customers for your various offers.

Sell the directories by mail-order or by direct mail, offering them at half price to those listed therein.

You can advertise that for xxx pounds you will circulate customers' names and addresses to firms eager to send them offers and programs. Sell the name lists to other dealers and firms who in turn mail offers to the list of customers. This saves money for the person wanting the offers, supplies the name list buyers with customers, and puts money in your pocket from both ends!

The names you compile as your business progresses are very valuable. You have customers for future mailing and can also sell or rent name lists to other mail-order dealers. Retain the original envelopes received so that you have proof of names, dates, addresses, etc.

You should start with only a small test list to determine if it is profitable. If it tests out reasonably well, then order a larger number of the same list. If this still proves out and the orders are pouring in with enough volume to cover all your costs and show a reasonable profit, then and only then, it should be safe to multiply your earnings by going all the way with the full list that is available.

Always remember that some lists will be completely worthless for your offer. You must test each list before committing mail-order "suicide". Be certain to choose the right category of names. If you are selling a novel you wouldn't want to mail to a list of opportunity seekers.

However, if it is a how-to-do-it type book, report, or folio, then a list of opportunity seekers may be even better than a list of known book buyers. Tests! The only way to know for sure.

If you study the many classified ads in the big national publications, you may get a better idea of what the leading companies in mail-order are doing and a better idea of how classified advertising works. If you have sufficient capital, some good pulling national magazines or tabloids are:

- *Woman's Own*
- *Family Circle*
- *BBC Gardeners World*
- *Radio Times*
- *Tatler*
- *Angling Times*

Many such magazine, tabloids and other good publications are available at your local newsagents, library or through mail-order. Most of these publications belong to organisations which promote a version of the Mail Order Protection Scheme (MOPS) and therefore have extremely strict guidelines concerning the advertisements they run. Many of them require a copy of the material you are selling with your ad and reserve the right not to print certain ads they feel may be injurious to the public or to the image of their publication.

Yes! You can start your own advertising and mailing business at home and keep your finances ahead of inflation, but be sure you are involved in the kind of program that gives you a reasonable chance to be a winner!

How to reach the hobby and collectors' markets

You can, if you are ambitious, start a mail-order business selling collectibles to hobbyists by mail. To begin, first find a hobby that appeals to you. Next, spend several weeks researching that hobby. Learn what collectors want and how much they are willing to pay for it. You should also know what other dealers are willing to pay for the merchandise which they sell. And, you must be willing to pay the same amounts.

note The first rule of mail-order selling is to sell what you yourself would buy.

Perhaps you already know exactly what you want to sell. If you have been collecting old valentines, then start a mail-order business buying and selling old valentines. Or stamps. Or comic books. To give you an idea of what collectors buy and sell by mail, here is a partial list of today's collectibles!

Advertising Cards	Autographs	Arrowheads
Antique Barbed Wire	Automobile Manuals	Beatles Items
Beer Labels	Belt Buckles	Boat Photograph
Buttons	Cartoon Books	Cigar Boxes
Playing Cards	Cigar Labels	Circus Posters
Children's Books	Coins	Comic Books
Cookbooks	Diaries	Dolls
Doll Clothes	Dog Pictures	Fishing Licences
Fruit Jar Labels	Gems, Minerals	Greeting Cards
Gun Catalogues	Hunting Licences	Licence Plates
Film Magazines	Maps	Menus
Military Medals	Newspapers	Old Magazines

Old Toys	Old Pencils	Old Calendars
Old Jewelry	Paper Currency	Phonograph Records
Political Buttons	Postcards	Railroad Books
Railroad Passes	Salt/Pepper Shakers	Stock Certificates
Stamps	Sheet Music	Theatre Programmes
Street Car Tokens	Thimbles	Train Photos
Valentines		

Once you select your field, start a file. Keep copies of all the ads selling your kind of merchandise. Also keep ads showing the dealers' buying prices. If price lists are offered in ads, send for them and study them. Make yourself an expert in your field.

Your next step is to look for merchandise in your own community. Here are some suggestions:

1. Attend flea markets and antique shows. Don't be afraid to make inquiries of dealers. They often have what they consider "junk" stashed away, assuming that it isn't of much value to anyone. I once discovered a fabulous stamp collection that way!

2. Browse charity and second hand shops.

3. Study car boot sale ads in your local newspaper. Visit any that sound promising. (Sometimes, it pays to telephone. They may be able to direct you to others who have exactly what you need!)

4. Place "Wanted to Buy" ads in your local newspaper. Be sure to list your phone number.

It is amazing what you can find in your local community if you work at it. If you can't find enough merchandise locally, run ads in the collector's magazines. Their rates are very low. And, you will soon discover that they are widely read!

Once you accumulate a decent stock of merchandise, you are ready to begin selling it. If there are publications specialising in your field, by all means advertise there. You have a ready-made audience! Also, run ads in the big hobby magazines.

Type a list of what you have and have a printer make a hundred or so copies for you. Hobbyists don't mind typewritten mimeographed or Xerox copies- it's half the fun of collecting. Then, run your ad. Your ad can merely offer your list to interested collectors free (or for a stamp, to weed out coupon clippers). Or, you can offer to make a sale straight from the ad. If you do the latter, stick in your price list with the merchandise. It will be read...eagerly!

TIP Try to locate any publication that deals with your field. Often, you can locate small mimeographed publications and newsletters that will give you all kinds of useful information.

Here are a few sample ads run by hobby dealers for your consideration:

Railway Timetables, 1940s Four Different – £4.00 postpaid.

Old Children's Books and Texts. Stamp for List.

85,000 Comic Books, Film Magazines, etc., 1900-1957. Catalogue £1.00 (Refundable).

Original Film Posters, Pressbooks, Stills, 1919-1975 Catalogue 50p.

Sleigh Bells! Stamp for list.

As you progress, you will learn continually. Most hobby dealers will tell you that they learn more from the collectors who buy from them than they could ever learn from any other source.

Below are some other hobby publications that may interest you. You can write to these publications and request a sample copy. However, it is a good idea to include postage when requesting copies from the publisher.

Definition:
Just in case you are not familiar with the phrase, "SAE" means "Self-addressed envelope."

Autoclassic Weekly, 60 Waldegrave Rd, Teddington, TW11

Ceramic Review, 21 Carnaby Street, London W1V

Complete Football International, 10 Leegate, London SE12

Cycling Today, 435-437 Coldharbour Lane, London SW9

Exchange & Mart Magazine, Lenning Hse, Masons Ave, Croydon CR0

Gift Buyer International, M1 Victoria Hse, Southampton Row, WC1B

Stamp Magazine, Link Hse, Dingwall Ave, Croydon CR9

Moving Pictures International, 151-153 Wardour Street, London W1V

Antiques Trade Gazette, 17 Whitcomb Street, London WC2H

Amateur Photographer, Kings Reach Tower, Stamford St, London SE1

Power tools for making more money

7

Chapter 7

Power tools for making more money

The mail-order catalogue

Perfection in a mail-order catalogue is like infinity—you can continually approach it but never quite reach it. In the case of many catalogues, however, it is not necessary to achieve perfection or even approach it very closely—in order to make the catalogue vastly more profitable than it is at present. Relatively small improvements can result in a more-than-proportionate enlargement of that all-important figure on the bottom line of the financial statement.

To make as many improvements as quickly as possible is probably the most profitable procedure. Even making each new catalogue a little better than the one that preceded it can produce substantial increases in sales per catalogue and in total sales over a period of time.

Following are suggestions that should help your catalogue do a better selling job for you. Whether you use all of them in connection with your next catalogue or adopt a few at a time in the course of producing several future catalogues, the ultimate result should be very noticeable and very gratifying.

Before you create your catalogue

• Look at your present catalogue with extremely cold, critical and unsympathetic eyes. Pick out all the faults—large or small—that you could find if you were no longer the owner of the catalogue but a nitpicking customer who was disappointed in his or her last purchase from you and is still sore about it. Such a review could be very enlightening—even if it should prove slightly embarrassing—and could make your new catalogue much more profitable.

> *note*
>
> Think of your catalogue as a means of helping your prospects accomplish something they want to accomplish or create an effect they want to create. Prepare your layouts, copy and illustrations accordingly.

• Put your "letterman" on your team. Review all incoming correspondence from customers and prospects during the last two years for comments, suggestions or criticisms that may be helpful in preparing your new catalogue. Screen all future correspondence of this nature as it arrives and place copies of the useful letters in a special file to be reviewed before starting your next catalogue.

• For each major type of product you sell, determine as many reasons as possible why different groups of prospects or customers buy or should buy this product. Arrange your groups of prospects or customers in order of importance. For each group, arrange the reasons for buying in order of their importance. Then arrange the reasons in order of importance to your total group of prospects or customers. Use the most important reasons as the basis for the copy and illustrations you use in this catalogue.

If there are significant differences in the primary reasons for purchasing different types of products, make the presentation for each specific type of product fit the product, using the same type of presentation for different types of products.

• If the preceding reasons indicate that different appeals are needed for different groups of prospects or customers, change the wrap-around, letter or introductory page of your catalogue to appeal to different groups, and separate your mailings accordingly.

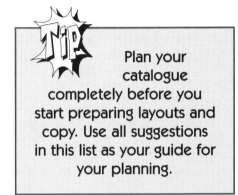

Plan your catalogue completely before you start preparing layouts and copy. Use all suggestions in this list as your guide for your planning.

• Attract new customers— reactivate dormant customers—and get bigger and better orders from present customers by adding new, exciting and extra pleasure to owning or using the types of products offered in your catalogue. For example, feature dramatic new items, unusual items, items that are especially timely, etc. Include unusual facts of interest about specific items.

• Add interest to your catalogue and give it a much longer life by including helpful information on how to use, operate and maintain your products—unusual uses, etc. This is information that customers can use to advantage and want to keep for future reference. Such information also increases customer confidence in your company which correspondingly increases the customer's inclination to buy from you.

• Determine whether items that were unprofitable or barely profitable in the present catalogue should be promoted more vigorously in the new catalogue or should be dropped and replaced by new products, Never keep an unprofitable product in your catalogue just because it is one of your favourites. If it doesn't sell, get rid of it!

• Give your company a distinct personality. Promote this personality in all future catalogues to make your company not "just another mail-order marketer," but a very special marketer in the minds of your prospects and customers.

When you create your new catalogue

Use the following to make your prospects want your products:

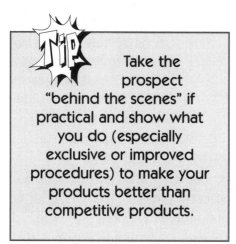

Take the prospect "behind the scenes" if practical and show what you do (especially exclusive or improved procedures) to make your products better than competitive products.

◆ Write your copy to tie in with and stimulate the specific reasons for buying discussed in the preceding section.

◆ Wherever possible show your prospects how your merchandise can accomplish the results desired by the prospects to a greater degree than competitive products. Prove it by citing results of lab tests, field tests, awards received, and other special recognitions—especially testimonials and case history stories, preferably with photographs. Give the prospect every possible incentive to buy from you rather than somebody else.

◆ Put special emphasis on your products and/or services which are exclusive or markedly superior to those of your competitors—and tell your readers WHY your products and/or services are superior!

◆ Make the most of new items the first time you offer them; they are only new once. Give them every opportunity to succeed saleswise by giving them preferred position and allowing adequate space for you to do a proper educational and selling job on them at the time they are introduced.

◆ Assure prospects that it is easy to use these products—that instructions are included with each order (if true) and/or are available in specific books or magazines (preferably obtainable from you). Cite case histories to prove how successful other customers were when using them.

◆ Tell prospects how to start using your merchandise properly and what other action should be taken—and when—or state that this information will be included with the shipment.

◆ If your products are bought primarily for pleasure or are considered a luxury or "non-necessity," help the prospect rationalise the value of the purchase.

Use the following procedures to make it as easy as possible for the prospect to make an accurate selection of the types of merchandise and the specific items of each type best suited for his or her purposes:

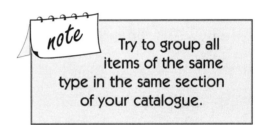

note

Try to group all items of the same type in the same section of your catalogue.

• Arrange the groups of items in their present or potential order of importance to you profitwise. Put the most important group at the front of your catalogue and the least important near the end of your catalogue (but not on the last three pages).

• Within each group, arrange the individual items in descending order of quality, price, popularity or promotional possibilities.

• Give the most important items the most valuable positions and extra space for copy and illustrations. Allocate positions and space to the other items in the order of their importance.

• If practicable, offer the same type of item in three different qualities—good, better and best—with different price ranges to match the differences in quality. Usually it is more effective to talk about the BEST quality first and the GOOD quality last.

• Use common copy to present features or qualities that are the same for all or most items of the same type.

• Use individual copy to talk about the features or qualities that make each specific item different from all or most of the other specific items in the group.

• In preparing the individual copy above, use "parallel construction" to help the prospect make a point-by-point comparison of the specific items as quickly, easily and accurately as possible.

Once the prospects have selected the merchandise they wish to buy, make it as easy as possible for them to order by using the next tips:

◆ Be sure your ordering information is easy to understand.

◆ Make your order form easy to use, with adequate space to write the necessary information.

> *note* Encourage prospects to order by phone with credit card details and encourage them to telephone for further information they may desire.

◆ Put in one or more extra order forms to make it easier for customers to order again.

◆ Offer a 24-hour phone-in service through an arrangement with a local telephone answering service. This is especially convenient for the customer who shops in your catalogue during evening or weekend hours.

Make it as easy as possible for customers to pay for their orders using the tips below:

• Offer credit card service on orders for a specified amount or more. By putting a minimum on credit card orders you will often increase the original order to at least that minimum amount. Credit card orders tend to be nearly double the size of cash orders.

- Make it easy to determine post and packing charges so they can be included in cash-with-order payments.

The following should help as order starters and sales stimulators:

- Use a wrap-around letter on the front of your catalogue to stimulate more orders and to do a selling job on the merchandise in the catalogue; also to make special appeals to special groups or call attention to merchandise in the catalogue of special interest to special groups.

Offer specials at intervals fixed throughout the catalogue to entice readers to start an order. Once they buy even one lonely item, they'll tend to order other items to go with it.

- Use the wrap-around to offer order starters (loss leaders or hot items to get prospects into the catalogue).

- Offer logical assortments of mixed or matched seasonal items to provide extra variety and pleasure at any given period of time. Make suggestions for these assortments and provide inducements for prospects to order them.

- Offer assortments of mixed or matched items designed for use during different seasons in order to provide variety and pleasure throughout the year (or most of it) instead of during just one season.

- Offer a free guide or plan for using each assortment above correctly and offer information on how to make the most effective overall use of the assortments.

- Offer a gift or discount for orders of certain sizes and use a stairstep graduated approach to increase the value of these discounts or gifts as the size of the order increases.

- Offer gift-shipping with gift cards.

•   Provide extra services such as "Seeker Service" for items not listed in the catalogue. Through extra service techniques you will make your customers more dependent on the information you provide and they will become more dedicated customers.

Stimulate promptness in ordering using the following tips:

♦ Use action incentives to spark early orders, such as premiums for ordering by a specified date; special offers for a limited time only; etc. When a time limit is involved, send a reminder (letter, promotional mailing, second catalogue, etc.) timed to arrive two weeks ahead of expiration date (as nearly as you can time it with current third class mail service).

> **TIP**
> Use teaser copy and cross-references throughout the catalogue to entice readers into other sections. This can be especially effective when related accessory items are sold.

♦ Mention frequently and prominently in your catalogue that anyone who orders merchandise from this catalogue will automatically receive the next catalogue free. If you wish, this offer can be modified to require the purchase of a specified amount during the life of the catalogue or by a specified date.

♦ Use the back cover of your catalogue for special offers; also the inside front and back covers and the pages facing the inside covers.

♦ Concentrate service information on a Service Page; locate it on a page conveniently adjacent to the order form; and use frequent cross-references to this page throughout the catalogue to stimulate extra page traffic.

♦ Humanise yourself and your catalogue by making it seem like the catalogue came from helpful, friendly people. If your business is truly a "family business" don't hide that fact.

♦ Watch your language! Avoid using technical "industry or business jargon" in your selling and service copy; keep legal phraseology to the absolute minimum in your guarantee.

♦ Make your entire catalogue harmonious in layout and copy style, but not monotonous. Include enough variety to keep the reader interested instead of bored.

♦ Give your catalogue a longer life by emphasising the length of time that you will be able to ship from it and suggesting that readers keep the catalogue for future reference.

♦ Ask for referrals from your satisfied customers; also names of friends who might like to receive a copy of the catalogue. Consider testing the "cluster concept" that neighbours are very similar and mail to your customers' next door neighbours.

♦ Sell subscriptions to your catalogue by providing a location on the catalogue for readers to remit 50 pence for a "full year's subscription to your catalogue." You can also suggest that they give a "gift subscription" to a friend very inexpensively (and thus pay for the catalogue you mail to the referral).

After you create your new catalogue

• Use the basic or major catalogue to establish the value and regular price of the merchandise. Use other, smaller catalogues or solo mailings to promote sales from the major catalogue or to provide special reasons for buying (reduced prices on individual items or special assortments, closeout, etc.).

> **note** Re-mail the same catalogue to your better customers 3 to 5 weeks after you mail it the first time.

• Ask the recipient to pass the catalogue along to an interested friend if the recipient already has a copy or is no longer interested in this type of merchandise.

> *note* Mail to your better customers monthly, featuring items carried in the catalogue—don't rely solely on the once-or-twice-a-year catalogue.

• Prepare an alternate cover for the catalogue and mail the same catalogue to your entire list several weeks later. You'll find it will do just about as well as the first mailing did.

• Use your catalogue as a package stuffer—enclose one with every order you ship. Your best prospect is the person who just placed an order with you and received prompt and safe delivery of the items ordered.

• Be prompt in acknowledging orders (with thanks), answering inquiries, shipping merchandise and making refunds or exchanges if necessary. Remember the old adage of that great retailer Marshall Field, "the customer is always right." Less than 2% of the population will intentionally try to take advantage of you. The other 98% are well worth cultivating.

Just as every good mail-order catalogue has something extra thrown in for good measure to make the customer happier, here's our extra one for good measure!

If you receive a change-of-address notice from one of your customers, immediately mail a copy of your catalogue addressed to "The New Residents at (the former address of the customer)" because the new residents probably have tastes and interests very similar to your customer—after all, they bought the same house! To give this mailing added power, you might tape a note onto the front cover of the book stating that "the Smiths used our catalogue regularly, maybe you'll find it equally useful."

Insider's guide to mail-order riches

With the millions of words printed every day about "How To Achieve Success," why aren't there more new millionaires?

It's simply because the people reading this "How-To" information don't understand what they read, or don't have the drive it takes to put what they've read into action. In truth, it seems that everyone wants to "find out how to become rich," but the people with the drive it takes to work a plan, are few and far between. The basics to getting rich can be stated as follows:

• **Control your investment.** This is the key to building a fortune from small capital. You must have the ability and knowledge to make the right moves at the right time, and above all, the innate talent it takes to always land on your feet and never be wiped out, regardless of the setbacks you may encounter.

• **Know how and where to buy for next to nothing**—or produce a product from scratch—and sell at a tremendous profit. With this ability, you can start with £100 or less, and sell it to someone else for much more than you paid for it. Then do it again, and keep on doing it until you have enough money to make substantial investments in other areas where your money will grow and prosper.

• **Buy things that appreciate in value.** In other words, learn to buy things that will grow in value as time goes on. Things such as collectibles, land, precious metals and stones. Think of the multiplication factor: You pay £10 for a copyright, sell 500 copies and you're off to a small fortune.

• **Be choosy.** Buy the original or pick a limited field. For instance, if you buy written material, buy from the author; or if you're into stamps or coins, work with just one country or type of coins/stamps.

• **Work the tax shelters.** To succeed in today's high taxation environment, you'll need to take advantage of every legitimate tax break. That may mean keeping a careful record of all business expenses. There are special rules for cars used for business, and if you work from home, you may be able to charge a proportion of your house expenses. Take care, though, because this may sacrifice a similar proportion of your capital gains tax exemption if you sell. Get sensible advice on your situation and follow it carefully; otherwise you might end up paying much more tax than you need.

> **TIP** Become an expert in your field of selling—know all there is to know about it. It takes time, effort, and energy, but the financial rewards are worth it.

• **Set goals and dedicate yourself to attaining those goals.** In just about any buy/sell program, you can set a rate of 20% net profit on each transaction, and work a five-time-a-year turnover. This doubles your capital each year. The net profit means just that—what is yours after all expenses and taxes are paid—so you have to get about 35 to 40% markup on each cycle. If you did your homework and are really an expert in your field, you'll often make profits of 200% and more on a single transaction, because real buys show up for the person with cash in hand. If you set a goal such as this, and follow this system starting with £100, in 10 years you may have over £50,000 in cash or its equivalent.

• **Learn to exercise patience.** This is the greatest attribute of a good hunter. In your field you'll look for bargains that can quickly be resold for a substantial profit. You have to learn the sources of the items you want to sell, how to spot the bargains, and then have the persistence to allow your investment to pay off for you.

• **Learn what to do with your riches.** When your capital has grown beyond the needs of your operation, put it to work. Get it into other investments that produce more capital and even more income. Pyramiding your investments brings you all the money you can use.

• **Keep your mouth shut!** The man with a method of making money, who understands what it can mean, keeps his mouth shut about it.

If this sounds like oversimplified hogwash, then you're missing the boat. Most people are so wrapped up in their own efforts—their own small little worlds—that they refuse to "picture and visualise" precisely how an idea or a program can or could be worked to amass a fortune. These same people, when the mood hits them, deal with, buy from, and pay an expert for the knowledge they refuse to understand or believe. The opportunity is there; all it needs is someone to grab it and run with it!

Managing your promotions and ads

8

Chapter 8

Managing your promotions and ads

What you'll find in this chapter:

- ➠ Writing compelling ads
- ➠ Ask for the sale
- ➠ Frequently asked questions and answers
- ➠ How to choose a dealer
- ➠ The dynamic principles of direct marketing

DEFINITION

Promotion advertising differs significantly from consumer franchise building advertising. The latter is long-term in nature and aimed at giving customers reasons to buy. Promotion advertising is short-term. It pushes for the order by providing incentives, coupons, rebates, premiums and contents.

The usual medium for promotion advertising is print. Some big-budget advertisers use broadcast (radio and television) to get consumers to look for their promotion advertising in their local newspapers.

As a rule, promotion advertising should be specific and should call only for the consumer to perform a desired action. Resist including extraneous points in the promotional ad. Focus on a simple call to action.

For example: Your ad copy may ask the readers to (1) Redeem this coupon and save £2, or (2) Buy two packs and get the third one free, or (3)

Fill out coupon and enter sweepstakes to win £100,000, or (4) Buy two of the products and receive a free gift worth £10. Most promotion events are price or added-value oriented campaigns.

 Final point: Do not make your redemption procedure complicated and confusing. Avoid having more than one time offers where the consumer is forced to use math in order to determine which ones make him/her save more money.

Your task is to make it easy for the consumer. Avoid making them decide. That's too much work.

How to write attention compelling advertisements

All sales begin with some form of advertising. To build sales, this advertising must be seen or heard by potential buyers, and cause them to react to the advertising in some way. The credit for the success, or the blame for the failure, of almost all ads reverts back to the ad itself.

Generally, the ad writer wants the prospect to do one of the following:

1)   Visit the shop to see and judge the product for himself, or immediately write a cheque and send for the merchandise being advertised.

2)   Phone for an appointment to hear the full sales presentation, or write for further information which amounts to the same thing.

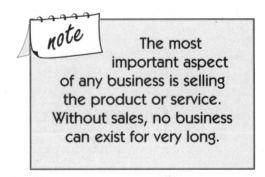

The most important aspect of any business is selling the product or service. Without sales, no business can exist for very long.

note

The bottom line in any ad is quite simple: To make the reader buy the product or service. Any ad that causes the reader to only pause in this thinking, to just admire the product, or to simply believe what's written about the product—is not doing its job completely.

In order to elicit the desired action from the prospect, all ads are written according to a simple master formula which is:

- attract the "attention" of your prospect

- "interest" your prospect in the product

- cause your prospect to "desire" the product

- demand "action" from the prospect

note

Never forget the basic rule of advertising copywriting: If the ad is not read, it won't stimulate any sale; if it is not seen, it cannot be read; and if it does not command or grab the attention of the reader, it will not be seen!

Most successful advertising copywriters know these fundamentals backwards and forwards. Whether you know them or you're just now being exposed to them, your knowledge and practice of these fundamentals determines the extent of your success as an advertising copywriter.

note The ad writer must know exactly what he wants the reader to do, and any that does not elicit the desired action is an absolute waste of time and money.

Classified ads

Classified ads are the ads from which all successful businesses are started. These small, relatively inexpensive ads, give the beginner an opportunity to advertise a product or service without losing their shirt if the ad doesn't pull or the people don't break the door down with demands for the product. Classified ads are written according to all the advertising rules. What is said in a classified ad is the same that's said in a larger, more elaborate type of ad, except in condensed form.

 To start learning how to write good classified ads, clip ten classified ads from ten different mail-order type publications—ads that you think are pretty good. Paste each of these ads onto a separate sheet of paper.

Analyse each of these ads: How has the writer attracted your attention—what about the ads keeps your interest—are you stimulated to want to know more about the product being advertised—and finally, what action must you take? Are all of these points covered in the ad? How strongly are you "turned on" by each of these ads?

Rate these ads on a scale of one to ten, with ten being the best according to the formula I gave you. Now, just for practice, without clipping the ads, do the same thing with ten different ads from a catalogue of your choice. In fact, every ad you see from now on, quickly analyse it, and rate it on your scale. If you practice this exercise on a regular basis, you'll soon quickly recognise the "Power Points" of any ad you see, and know whether an ad is good, bad or otherwise, and what makes it so.

Practice for an hour each day, write the ads you've rated 8, 9 and 10 exactly as they were written. This gives you the feel of the fundamentals and style necessary in writing classified ads.

 Your next project is to pick out what you consider to be the ten worst ads you can find in the classifieds sections. Clip these out and paste them onto a sheet of paper so you can work on them.

Read these ads over a couple of times, and then beside each of them, write a short comment stating why you think it's bad: Lost in the crowd, doesn't attract attention—doesn't hold the reader's interest—nothing special to make the reader want to own the product—no demand for action.

You probably already know what's coming next, and that's right. Break out those pencils, rubbers and scratch paper—and start rewriting these ads to include the missing elements.

Each day for the next month, practice writing the ten best ads for an hour, just the way they were originally written. Pick out ten of the worst ads, analyse those ads, and then practice rewriting those until they measure up to doing the job they were intended to do.

Once you're satisfied that the ads you rewrote are perfect, go back to each ad and cross out the words that can be eliminated without detracting from the ad. Classified ads are almost always finalised in the style of a telegram.

> *note* Practice, and keep at it, over and over, every day—until the formula, the idea, and the feel of this kind of ad writing becomes second nature to you. This is the ONLY WAY to gain expertise in writing good classified ads.

EXAMPLE: I'll arrive at 2 o'clock tomorrow afternoon, the 15th. Meet me at Brown's. All my love, Jim.

EDITED FOR SENDING: Arrive 2pm—15th—Brown's. Love, Jim.

CLASSIFIED AD: Save on your food bills! Reduced prices on every shelf in the store! Stock up now while supplies are complete! Come on in today, to The Camden Co-Op!

EDITED FOR PUBLICATION: Save on Food! Everything bargain priced! Limited Supplies! Hurry! Camden Co-Op!

It takes dedicated and regular practice, but you can do it. Simply recognise and understand the basic formula—practice reading and writing the good ones—and rewriting the bad ones to make them better.

Display advertisements

DEFINITION

A *display or space ad* differs from a classified ad because it has a headline, layout, and because the style isn't telegraphic. However, the fundamentals of writing the display or space ad are exactly the same as for a classified ad. The basic difference is that you have more room in which to emphasise the "master formula."

Most successful copywriters rate the headline and/or the lead sentence of an ad as the most important part. In reality, you should do the same. After all, when your ad is surrounded by hundreds of other ads, and information or entertainment, what makes you think anyone is going to see your ad?

> **CAUTION**
>
> If you don't capture the attention of your reader with your headline, anything beyond is useless effort and wasted money.

The truth is, they're not going to see your ad unless you grab their attention and entice them to read what you have to say. Your headline, or lead sentence when no headline is used, has to make it more difficult for your prospect to ignore or pass over, than to stop and read your ad.

Successful advertising headlines—in classified ads, your first three to five words serve as your headline—are written as promises, either implied or direct. The former promises to show you how to save money, make money, or attain a desired goal. The latter is a warning against something undesirable.

Example of a promise: *Are You Ready To Become A Millionaire—In Just 18 Months?*

Example of a warning: *Do You Make These Mistakes In English?*

In both examples, I posed a question as the headline. Headlines that ask a question seem to attract the reader's attention almost as surely as a moth is to a flame. Once they see the question, they just can't seem to keep from reading the rest of the ad to find out the answer.

"You'll be the envy of your friends" is another kind of reader appeal to incorporate in your headline when appropriate. The appeal has to do with basic psychology: everyone wants to be well thought of, and consequently, reads the body of your ad to find out how to gain the respect and accolades of their friends.

 Wherever and whenever possible, use colloquialisms or words not usually found in advertisements. The idea is to shock or shake readers out of their reverie and cause them to take notice of your ad. Most of the headlines you see each day have a certain sameness with just the words rearranged. Readers may see these headlines with their eyes, but their minds fail to focus on them because there's nothing different or out of the ordinary to arrest attention.

> The best headline questions are those that challenge the reader, involve self esteem, and do not allow the reader to dismiss your question with a simple yes or no.

Example of colloquialism: *Are You Developing a POT BELLY?*

Another attention-grabber kind of headline is the comparative pricegasines headline: *Three For Only £3, Regularly £3 Each!* Still another of the "tried and proven" kind of headlines is the specific question: *Do You Suffer From These Symptoms?* And of course, if you offer a strong guarantee, you should say so in your headline: *Your Money Refunded, If You Don't Make £100,000 Your First Year.*

"How To" headlines have a very strong basic appeal, but in some instances, they're better used as book titles than advertising headlines. Another approach with a very strong reader appeal is the "who else wants in on the finer things?" The psychology here is the need of everyone to belong to a group—complete with status and prestige motivations.

Whenever, and as often as possible, use the word "you" in your headline, and throughout your copy. After all, your ad should be directed to "one" person, and the person reading your ad wants to feel that you're talking to them personally, not everyone who lives on their street.

Personalise, and be specific! You can throw the teachings of your English teacher's out the window, and the rules of "third person, singular" or whatever else tends to inhibit your writing. Whenever you sit down to write advertising copy intended to pull the orders—sell the product—you should picture yourself in a one-on-one situation and "talk" to your readers just as if you were sitting across from them at your dining room table. Say what you mean, and sell the reader on the product. Be specific. Ask if these are the things that bother them—are these the things they want—and, they are the ones you want to buy the product.

> **TIP** Your ad should convey the feeling of excitement and movement, but should not tire the eyes or disrupt the flow of the message you are trying to present.

The layout you devise for your ad, or the frame you build around it, should also command attention. Either make it so spectacular that it stands out like lobster at a chilli dinner, or so uncommonly simple that it catches the reader's eye because of its very simplicity. It's also important that you don't get cute with a lot of unrelated graphics and artwork.

Any graphics or artwork you use should be relevant to your product, its use and/or the copy you wrote about it. Graphics should not be used as artistic touches, or to create an atmosphere. Any illustrations with your ad should compliment the selling of your product, and prove or substantiate specific points in your copy.

Once you have the reader's attention, the only way you are going to keep it is by quickly and emphatically telling the reader what your product will do for him.

Your potential buyer doesn't care in the least how long it's taken you to produce the product, how long you are in business, or how many years you spent learning your craft. The buyer wants to know specifically how they are going to benefit from the purchase of your product.

> *note* Generally, wants fall into one of the following categories: Better health, more comfort, more money, more leisure time, more popularity, greater beauty, success and/or security.

Even though you have your reader's attention, you must follow through with an enumeration of the benefits they can gain. In essence, you must reiterate the advantages, comfort and happiness they'll enjoy—as you implied in your headline.

Mentally picture your prospect—determine their wants and emotional needs—put yourself in their shoes, and ask yourself: If I were reading this ad, what are the things that would appeal to me? Write your copy to appeal to your reader's wants and emotional needs/ego cravings.

Remember, it's not the safety features that sold cars for the past 50 years—or the need of transportation—it was, and almost certainly will be the advertising writer's recognition of people's wants and emotional needs/ego cravings. Visualise your prospect, recognise his wants and satisfy them. Writing good advertising copy is nothing more or less than knowing "who" your buyers are; recognising what they want; and then telling them how your product will fulfil each of those wants. Remember this because it's one of the vitally important keys to writing advertising copy that will do the job you intend for it to do.

The "desire" portion of your ad is where you present the facts of your product; create and justify your prospect's conviction, and cause him to demand "a piece of the action" for himself.

It's vitally necessary that you present proven facts about your product because survey results show that at least 80% of the people reading your ad—especially those reading it for the first time—tend to question its authenticity.

So, the more facts you can present in the ad, the more credible your offer. As you write this part of your ad, always remember that the more facts about the product you present, the more product you'll sell.

> **Tip**
> People want facts as reasons, and/or excuses for buying a product—to justify to themselves and others that they were not "taken" by a slick copywriter.

It's like the girl who wants to marry the guy her father calls "good-for-nothing." Her heart—her emotions—tell her yes, but she needs to nullify the seed of doubt lingering in her mind—to rationalise her decision to go on with the wedding.

In other words, the "desire" portion of your ad has to build belief and credibility in the mind of your prospect. It has to assure your prospect of their good judgement in the final decision to buy—furnish evidence of the benefits you promised—and afford a safety net in case anyone should question their decision to buy.

Once you establish a belief in this manner, logic and reasoning are used to support it. People believe what they want to believe. Your reader wants to believe your ad if they read it through this far—it is up to you to support this initial desire.

> **note**
> People tend to believe the things that appeal to their individual desires, fears and other emotions.

note Study your product and everything about it—visualise the wants of your prospective buyers—dig up the facts. You'll almost always find plenty of facts to support the buyer's reasons for buying.

Here is where you use results of tests conducted, growing sales figures to prove increasing popularity, and user testimonials or endorsements. It's also important that you present these facts—test results, sales view, and not that of the manufacturer.

Before you end this portion of your ad and get to your demand for action, summarise everything you presented thus far. Draw a mental picture for your potential buyer. Let the reader imagine owning the product. Induce them to visualise all of the benefits you promised. Give them the keys to seeing themselves richer, enjoying luxury, having time to do whatever they would like to do, with all of their dreams fulfiled.

This can be handled in one or two sentences, or spelled out in a paragraph or more, but it is the absolute ingredient you must include prior to closing the sale. Study all the sales presentations you ever heard— look at every winning ad—this is the element included in all of them that actually makes the sale for you. Remember it, use it, and don't try to sell anything without it.

> *note*
>
> Plan your advertisement so it has a powerful impact upon those who are "hardest" to sell. Unlike face-to-face selling, we cannot in printed advertising come to a "trial close" in our sales talk—in order to see if those who are easier to sell will welcome the dotted line without further persuasion.

As Victor Schwab puts it so succinctly in his best selling book, *How To Write A Good Advertisement:* Every one of the fundamentals in the "master formula" is necessary. Assume you are talking to the hardest ones to sell to and that the more thoroughly your copy sells both to the hard and the easily sold, the better chance you have against the competition. Also, you are now less dependent upon the usual completely ineffective follow through on advertising effort which takes place at the sales counter.

Ask for action! Demand the money!

Lots of ads are beautiful, almost perfectly written, and quite convincing—yet, they fail to ask for or demand action from the reader. If you want the reader to have your product, then tell them so and demand that they send money now! Unless you enjoy entertaining your prospects with your beautiful writing skills, always demand that they complete the sale now, by taking action now—by calling a telephone number and ordering, or by writing their cheque and rushing it to the post office.

note

Once you have the buyer on the hook, land him! Don't let the buyer get away!

One of the most common and best methods of moving the reader to act now is written in some form of the following:

All of this can be yours! You can start enjoying this new way of life immediately, simply by sending a cheque for £XX! Don't put it off, then later wish you had gotten in on the ground floor! Make out that cheque now, and "be IN on the ground floor!" Act now, and as an "early-bird" buyer, we'll include a big bonus package—absolutely free, simply for acting immediately! You win all the way! We take all the risk! If you are not satisfied, simply return the product and we quickly refund your money! Do it now! Get that cheque on its way to us today, and receive the big bonus package! After next week, we won't be able to include the bonus as a part of this fantastic deal, so act now! The sooner you act, you more you win!

Offering a reward of some kind almost always stimulates the prospect to take action. However, in mentioning the reward or bonus, be very careful that you don't end up receiving primarily requests for the bonus with mountains of requests for refunds on the product to follow. The bonus should be mentioned only casually if you are asking for product orders; and with lots of fanfare only when you are seeking inquiries.

Too often copywriters, in their enthusiasm to pull in a record number of responses, confuse the reader by "forgetting about the product," and devoting their entire space allotted for the "demand for action" to sending for the bonus. Any reward offered should be closely related to the product, and a bonus offered only for immediate action on the part of the potential buyer.

 Specify a time limit. Tell your prospect that he must act within a certain time limit or lose out on the bonus, face probably higher prices, or even the withdrawal of your offer. This is always a good hook to get action.

Any kind of guarantee you offer always helps you produce action from the prospect. Be sure you state the guarantee clearly and simply. Make it so easy to understand that even a child would not misinterpret what you are saying.

note The more liberal you can make your guarantee, the more product orders you will receive.

The action you want your prospect to take should be easy—clearly stated—and devoid of any complicated procedural steps, or numerous directions to follow.

Picture your prospects, sitting very comfortably, half-watching the television as they idly flip through a magazine. They notice your ad, read through it, and are sold on your product. Now, what do they do?

Remember, they're very comfortable—you grabbed their attention, sparked interest, painted a picture of enjoying a new kind of satisfaction, and they are ready to buy.

Anything and everything you ask or cause them to do is going to disrupt this aura of comfort and contentment. Whatever they must do had better be simple, quick and easy!

Tell them without any ifs, ands or buts, what to do—*fill out the coupon, include your cheque for the full amount, and send it in to us today!* Make it as easy as you possibly can—simple and direct. By all means, make sure your name and address are on the order form they are supposed to complete and mail in to you—as well as just above it. People sometimes fill out a coupon, tear it off, seal it in an envelope and don't know where to send it. The easier you make it for them to respond, the more responses you'll get!

There you have it, a complete short course on how to write ads that pull more orders for you—sell more of your product for you. It's important to learn "why" ads are written as they are—to understand and use the "master formula" in your own ad writing endeavours.

You must keep yourself up-to-date, aware of, and in-the-know about the other guys—their innovations, style, changes, and the methods they use to sell products.

By conscientiously studying good advertising copy, and practicing writing ads of your own, now that you have the knowledge to understand what makes advertising copy work, you should be able to quickly develop your copywriting abilities to produce order-pulling ads for your own products. Even so, once you do become proficient in writing ads for your own products, you must never stop "noticing" how ads are written, designed and put together by other people. To stop learning would be comparable to shutting off from the rest of the world.

The best ad writers are people in touch with the world in which they live. Every time they see a good ad, they clip it out and save it. Regularly, they review what makes them good, and why they work. There's no school in the country that can give you the same kind of education and expertise so necessary in the field of ad writing. On-the-job training—study and practice—that's what it takes—and, if you have that burning ambition to succeed, you can do it too!

Questions & answers

1) *What's the most profitable way to use classifieds?*

Classifieds are best used to build your mailing list of qualified prospects. Use classified ads to offer a free catalogue, booklet or report relative to your product line.

2) *What can you sell "directly" from classifieds?*

Generally, anything and everything, so long as it doesn't cost more than £5.00 which is about the most people will pay in response to an offer in the classifieds. These types of ads are great for pulling inquiries such as: Write for further information; Send £3, get two for the price of one; Dealers wanted, send for product info and a real money-maker's kit!

3) *What are the best months of the year to advertise?*

All twelve months of the year! Responses to your ads during some months will be slower in accumulating, but by keying your ads according to the month they appear, and a careful tabulation of your returns from each keyed ad, you will see that steady year-round advertising will continue to pull orders for you, regardless of the month it's published. I've personally received inquiries and orders from ads placed as long as 2 years previous to the date of the response!

4) *How can I decide where to advertise my product?*

First of all, determine who your prospective buyers are. Then do a little market research. Talk to your friends, neighbours and people at random who might fit this profile. Ask if they would be interested in a product such as yours, and then ask which publications they read. Next, go to your public library for a listing of the publications of this type from the British Rate & Data Directory.

Make a list of the addresses, circulation figures, reader demographics and advertising rates. To determine the true costs of your advertising and decide which is the better buy, divide the total audited circulation figure into the cost for a one inch ad: £10 per inch with a publication showing 10,000 circulation would be 10,000 into £10 or 10 per thousand. Looking at the advertising rates for *Exchange & Mart*, you take 42,500 into £15 for an advertising rate of less than 3/10th of one cent per thousand. Obviously, your best buy in this case would be *Exchange & Mart* because of the lower cost per thousand.

Write and ask for sample copies of the magazines in which you have tentatively chosen to place your advertising. Look over their advertising. Be sure they don't or won't put your ad in the *"gutter,"* which is the inside column next to the binding. How many other mail-order type ads are they carrying? You want to go with a publication that's busy, not one that has only a few ads.

To properly test your ad, let it run through at least three consecutive issues of any publication. If your responses are small, try a different publication. Then, if your responses are still small, look at your ad and think about rewriting it for greater appeal and pulling power. In many instances, it's the ad that's at fault and not the publication's pulling power!

How to choose a print and mail dealer

A direct mail campaign is expensive! There are many ways to cut the cost of your mailings: bulk mail, SAEs, and many other ways. One of the best ways to lower your mailing costs, though, is by using a print and mail dealer. Print and mail dealers do exactly what their name describes. They can take your ads, usually A4 flyers, print them and mail them to names drawn from a mailing list. Their services are quite inexpensive, sometimes costing close to what your local printer would charge for printing alone.

> **note** The best mailing lists in mail-order are made up of people who have bought within the past 30 days. Anything over 90 days old shouldn't be used. Reputable print & mail dealers shouldn't have a problem with providing this information.

A print & mail business runs something like this: When the dealer receives an order from a customer (for example, 1,000 A4 flyers, printed and mailed), they will print the flyers on one side of the paper, with THEIR flyer on the back.

Thus, anyone who receives the customer's flyer also gets the dealer's flyer. This cuts their advertising costs.

Then, they assemble a group of different orders together into one mailing. This could be as little as two pages, to as large as 50 pages. These are bulk mailed to names drawn from a mailing list, usually of opportunity seekers or mail-order enthusiasts. They could also be mailed out to those who responded to ads the print and mail dealer placed.

How can you be sure a print and mail dealer will do a good job for you? There are four things you should do when dealing with a print and mail dealer for the first time. The first two should be done when shopping for a dealer; the other two are done after your first order is placed.

First, send the dealer a request to be added to their mailing list. You should then receive the next mailing. If you don't want to wait for a bulk mail, send a few first-class stamps, and you'll probably receive it quicker.

Look through the mailing and observe the printing quality. Is it smudgy, smeary and hard to read, or is it crisp and clear? If the printing straight, or crooked? Keep in mind, the quality of the mailing you receive will probably be the quality of YOUR flyer if you use this dealer. Do this for a number of dealers and you will quickly be able to determine which will give you the best print quality.

Second, find out what type of names the dealer is mailing to, and where they come from. For best results, make sure the dealers' names are fresh.

Third, when you place your printing order, request a checking copy. This is a copy of the bulk mailing, sent to you. You can then see exactly how your printing came out, the other offers surrounding yours, and your position in the mailing. Finally, also request proof of mailing. When you send a bulk mailing at the post office, they provide you with a receipt listing the date and the number mailed. Request that a photocopy of this be mailed to you with your checking copy. Not all dealers will do this, but the reputable ones should have no problem with it.

If everything looks good, and you sent a good offer to be distributed, you should get favourable results.

note This report is not meant to say that a lot of print & mail dealers are disreputable. Most use high quality lists and produce top notch printing. Otherwise, they would never get return customers. Just be sure that you "look before you leap."

22 dynamic principles of direct marketing

1) There are four important elements in a **"Direct Mail Package"** and close attention must be paid to each: (Before anything, of course, comes the essential "idea" since the conceptual strategy is still key.)

- *the graphics* (carrier) which must be opened by reader—i.e, "what does it look like?"

- *the offer:* the way the proposition is phrased—i.e "what's the deal?"

- *the copy:* the compelling description that gets the reader to buy or act—i.e. "how is it said?"

- *the list:* the targeted audience most likely willing to buy or act—i.e. "who is it sent to?"

2) **The list.** Perhaps the most important element is the list. Others believe copy is most important, but don't let ranking bother you since each element is important. Take all reasonable steps to get, use and keep the most accurate and up-to-date lists possible to increase your margin of success. Set up a system to add names and keep 'em current.

3) **Heed "Daly's Law"**—"Everything takes longer and costs more!" So, it's wise to start the project in ample time to make all elements come   together in an easy manner. Use "reverse timetable" to plot what needs to be done and when. For instance, you probably need to order lists first. Then, don't forget the envelopes, printed stock, other enclosures, etc. Allow time for delivery and return action plus follow-up mailings.

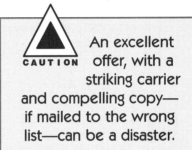

An excellent offer, with a striking carrier and compelling copy—if mailed to the wrong list—can be a disaster.

4) **Test.** If possible, test some or all portions of your program so you can alter methods if needed. Direct Mail is a demanding taskmaster, so if it fails it's probably you who missed somewhere, not the medium.

5) **Heed basic principles of writing.** Compelling Direct Mail copy only seems simple, so don't be deceived. Write to a single person in simple, straightforward manner—yet with style. Long copy is not necessarily bad, in fact it can outpull short copy. Focus on main message you intend to convey. Never forget you want action to occur...NOW. Be sure copy answers for the always-asked question: "What's in it for me?" Always keep the reader's perceived needs in mind. Do the necessary research to help determine them.

6) **Closely analyse your potential markets** and your offer so you can hone lists and copy to target your approach. Though you mail by the thousands, remember Direct Mail is more akin to a rifle than a shotgun. Write your copy to be read by one person at a time.

For success remember the 3 "S's" of successful copy are: (1) Simplicity, (2) Sincerity, (3) Serenity.

7) **Remember Direct Mail is a substitute sales representative.** Where an in-person sales representative can immediately answer prospects' questions and overcome objections when raised, direct mail copy must anticipate all aspects and insure logical points are covered.

8) **Incorporate an action device**—coupon, order form, reply card or envelope, phone number—to make it easy for recipient to take desired action. Repeatedly tell recipient what action you want and make it simple to do. Put nothing in the way of getting an order or response. Use all action devices cited.

9) **A letter almost always works better** in a Direct Mail package than a package—even a catalogue—without a letter. Don't worry if the letter repeats what's in the catalogue, brochure or order form. It's there for a different purpose. The sales letter is a one-to-one communication to explain and sell, to get the recipient to act. The postscript is often the most-read part of the letter.

10) If all elements of the package are good, **it is imperative that repeat mailings be made.** It's difficult to wear out a good list and, unless mailings are overdone, you can't wear out your welcome. Let statistical probabilities and the laws of economics work in your favour rather than allow difference about making frequent mailings deter you. A common error is not to mail often enough or to a wider list.

11) **Keep detailed records of everything you do.** Follow a "systems approach" so you know what happened, when and why. That way you can repeat successes and avoid failures. Sometimes the difference of a tenth of a percent or less is all it takes to turn a marginal performer into a winner.

12) **Study all elements of your package so you can know what's**

> **Tip** Save, subdivide and study the good Direct Mail. You get to learn what to do—and maybe what not to do. Remember some of the things that appeal may, in fact, be "tests" that, when results are known, are failures. Never underestimate the need for simplicity and complete honesty.

working. Is it the price? The geography? The timing? The phrasing of the offer? The list? The copy? The product? Which of those myriad elements, in combination or without one element, makes the critical difference in the return? Analyse your records closely and continually until you know why you're winning and can repeat success.

13)   **Keep current with changing postal rules, rates, regulations and procedures.** Regularly monitor your procedures to insure you're in full compliance.

14) **People who take actions by mail are different from those who don't.** Thus it is wise to isolate them so you can easily remail with new or different offers. Remember the axiom:"People who buy by mail...buy by mail...buy by mail..." Best lists are of mail buyers of similar products or services who recently purchased in same price range.

> **note** Royal Mail has produced an extremely useful booklet on Direct Mail. Ask for your free copy as soon as possible. It will help tremendously!

15) **Do what's necessary to make your mail stand out**, even "look peculiar" since it has to fight all types of competition. Clever teaser copy on outside of carrier can work wonders.

16) **Wise mail merchants work at differentiating between "suspects," "prospects," and (best of all) "customers."** Once they can

distinguish names on lists among those three categories they are able to achieve cost efficiencies that novices can only dream about.

17) **Testimonials can be effective promotional tools**, especially if they're heartfelt and cogently express what the average user might feel about a product or service. They're even better when offered by celebrities or persons well-known to the audience. Treat testimonials like the jewels they are and gather more.

18) **There's no such thing as a normal percentage of return** that's universally applicable across a wide range of products and services but, over time and by keeping careful records, you can determine what some norms are for your offer (s). Your goal then is to "beat your best"...if only by 1/2 or 1/4 of a percent!

19) In producing Direct Mail programs these seven words may be cliche—but, only because they're true: **"Nothing is as simple as it seems."** Exercise continual care at every step of the planning and conceptual stage. Any step here can become critical if close attention isn't paid to what's happening. "To *error* is human." Yes, I'm aware of the error, but that's the exact spelling of a sign I spotted in printer's window. I reproduce it now to emphasise how vital it is that extreme care be given to this side of production. Proofreading in a professional manner is essential.

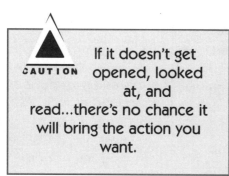

CAUTION

If it doesn't get opened, looked at, and read...there's no chance it will bring the action you want.

20) Long ago I was cautioned to **be aware of these two "sinful" acronyms: KISS and CIPU**. The first, "Keep It Simple, Sweetie" describes how to tell your message, while the second cautions us to avoid lapsing into business or industrial jargon which "we" understand, but most everyone else doesn't. CIPU stands for "Clear If Previously Understood."

21) While the Power of Mail will long be with us (even though the

nature of the Postal Service might change), **wise direct mailers see themselves practicing in the fields of "Direct Marketing" or "Direct Response."** They become knowledgeable of the synergistic value from use of print media (magazines, space ads, newspaper inserts, etc.) as well as electronic media (radio and/or TV) to supplement their mail promotional efforts. The combination can be powerful.

22) **Continually study and be alert to what's happening in this dynamic medium.** It may seem that not much is new, when in fact, there are subtle, but important shifts, in many of the areas delineated in each of the four elements cited in Principle #1.

Build a mailing list that gets results

9

Chapter 9

Build a mailing list that gets results

Do you want to receive orders every day of the year? You can if you have a mailbox or post office box and if you sell something that people want. The "secret" is explained in this chapter so you can profit from what I learned the hard way in mail-order.

DEFINITION

Most dealers believe that a profit cannot be made unless items with big price tags are offered to the buying public. This is far from the truth. To keep orders coming in on a regular basis you must use *good will* and *leader* items. These are good pulling offers that keep money coming in daily to your mailbox. In an average week leader items selling for under a pound or postage stamps can bring in dozens and dozens of orders. Offering valuable information, for example, with price tags that build customer interest can create regular repeat buyers for your offers.

For years in America I offered information for 50 cents, $1.00 and/or postage stamps and found that these were really big sellers that built customer trust, plus a valuable mailing list I could use over and over again.

Most of my offers are short mini-folios containing a few thousand words of helpful or money-saving information. The cost is only a few pennies to print. My profit margin is enormous even with the present cost of printing envelopes and postage. My profit margin is maintained by asking for self addressed stamped envelopes. Customers who send me the small amounts usually send larger orders later. With each out-going order, I include my other money making offers. They get a "free ride" with the original report. My repeat orders were always above 50%.

> **note** Selling information for such small amounts may not seem like much profit to you, but you are getting valuable names of buyers for your own mailing list plus you can sell these names to other dealers for a profit.

You can get BIG response to your advertising if you just use your imagination. If you have a piece of material that has not made the rounds in mail-order publications, put the material into your own words and sell it. Simply sell a good piece of information and watch the money roll in every day in your mailbox. This is how to keep your mailbox full of orders 365-days-a-year!

Inquiry, prospect and suspect names for your mailing list

Your lists of inquiry, prospect and suspect names are very important to the long-term success of your business. These are the names that you try to convert into loyal customers. This process can be the key to your growing business or organisation.

Prospecting as an "investment" philosophy

Your customer list should be considered one of your most valuable assets. Unfortunately, customers sometimes move, die, go out of business, or just decide to take their business elsewhere. You must continue to replenish and build this list by prospecting for new customers if you want your business to grow or even just to survive.

Prospecting successfully does not come easily—or inexpensively—which is why it should be considered an investment. In comparison to your results from mailings to your customers, your response from mailing to prospects will be much lower. By the time you add the costs of prospect lists, along with production costs and postage, you almost surely lose money in your attempt to recruit new customers. This loss is called *"front-end cost"* or an *"acquisition cost."*

> **Definition:**
> Prospecting—attempting to convert potential buyers into customers—is a means of investing in the future of your organisation.

DEFINITION

Your profit from prospecting comes on the "back-end," once you acquire these new accounts. If your new customers continue to shop from you or use your service or renew their membership to the point where your back-end profits cover your front-end costs, you've succeeded. Of course, that primarily depends on how you handle the initial contact(s) and whether you establish a good long-term relationship with the new customer.

Defining the characteristics of potential customers

Where should you look to find your potential new customers? The sources you use to develop the names of your inquiries, prospects and suspects will depend on your understanding of current customers and your business.

You want to select and maintain the names of individuals (or businesses) sharing the characteristics of your best current customers. You already know what those characteristics are. When you created your customer database, you made decisions about which data to capture for each of the customer names on the mailing list.

For example, you might determine that your best customers live in a definable geographic area or attained a certain income or gross revenue level. They may have a specific family or organisational structure. Or, they may have interests or regularly pursue activities that make them good prospects for your product or service. You want to first pursue prospects with those same characteristics.

Finding sources for prospect names

There are two different ways to build a list for prospecting:

1) Through direct prospecting (also called *one-step*).

2) Through lead generation (commonly known as *two-step*).

DEFINITION

With a *one-step process*, you are trying to sell your product or service directly to the prospect via a list of people or firms you think are likely to purchase. Once the sale is closed, the prospect becomes a customer.

DEFINITION

In a *two-step system*, first try to get prospects to indicate their interest through generating an inquiry about the product or service. You can then target your mailing or other sale efforts to names that have a greater likelihood of responding, and also have a certain identified need which can be fulfiled by your product or service.

There are many sources you can use to develop lists of potential customers. Here, we are going to describe some of the most productive sources for inquiry, prospect and suspect names.

Sources for inquiry names

Inquiries are people or firms that present themselves to you by asking about your product, service or organisation in general. They are better potential customers than "cold" prospects or suspects because they expressed some interest in your organisation and already responded in some way.

> **note**
> If you are developing a program to recruit inquiries, you must first plan how you are going to respond to the inquirer.

A list of inquiries and leads does no good unless you have a way to convert them into customers. Two factors determine how many inquiries convert to customers: (1) speed of response and (2) offer given to the inquiry. The faster you get your sales pitch into the inquirer's hands, the more likely you'll get a future order. The longer you wait, the more your results are reduced. Also, since you already invested money in this lead when generating the inquiry, make sure to present your best possible offer. The most common problem with inquiry programs is that inquirers are not treated with the care and attention they deserve.

Actively soliciting inquiries

You should not wait passively for people to inquire about your organisation. You can actively invite inquiries. Below are descriptions of some of the more common ways to do this:

Media Advertising

An advertising programme can stimulate inquiries about your organisation in addition to selling your product or service. Your advertising programme can be quite simple if you want only local exposure:

- Place classified advertisements in area newspapers.

- Buy ad space in community newsletters.

- Use a display ad for Yellow Pages listing.

- Purchase time on local radio programmes.

If your audience is national, generate inquiries by:

◆ Placing advertisements in national magazines.

DEFINITION

◆ Buying space in *card decks*. A card deck is a group of promotional postcards sent to a set of defined prospects. The cards are usually wrapped in plastic, may offer products or information, and always include a way for the prospect to respond.

Whether using your advertising to sell a product or service or simply to urge people to inquire about the organisation (or a combination of both), always include some way for them to respond. Coupons, a tear-off card and a freephone number are often used to make it easy to inquire. Also, the advertisement should always feature your organisation name, address and phone number prominently.

> *note* Whichever media you choose to advertise in, make sure it serves the same audience you want to attract.

A word of caution about the method through which inquiries can respond. If you make it too easy to respond, you may get inquiries from people with no interest in your organisation, but who simply like to fill out forms and/or receive mail.

It costs money to respond to inquiries (especially if these are leads for salespeople), so make sure your objectives are clear before designing your programme. Are you looking to obtain as many names as possible or do you want to receive inquiries from "highly qualified" leads only?

There are a number of ways to qualify inquiries. Roughly speaking, the more difficult (or expensive) it is to respond, the more likely it is that the inquiry has a true interest in your organisation. For example:

- A few short questions on the response form may deter people who aren't really interested in your organisation. In any case, YOU can qualify inquiries based on the information given and choose to add them to the list or not.

- A freephone number may produce a greater proportion of "non-qualified" responses than would a phone call for which the inquirer must pay. (The same principle holds true for reply-paid vs. unstamped response form.)

Trade show exhibiting

Companies exhibit at trade shows for a number of reasons: to sell a product, to talk to customers, to build name identification, etc. However, one benefit of trade show exhibiting which is often ignored is to talk to prospective customers and collect their names for follow-up with future mailings.

If you want to exhibit at trade shows solely for the purpose of generating leads, first answer the following questions:

- ◆ What is the expense involved in exhibiting? Registration fee? Materials for the booth? Travel costs?

- ◆ Does the type of business or individual who fits your customer profile attend?

◆ How many businesses or individuals attend?

◆ What response rates would you need to pay for the costs of exhibiting?

◆ Is your product or service appropriate for the show?

◆ Are there other benefits to exhibiting at the show, such as selling products, increasing awareness of your organisation, creating goodwill, or gathering information about the competitors?

 note If you decide to exhibit at a trade show, you should have a well thought out method for collecting qualified prospect names.

Too many trade show exhibitors overlook this necessary step. At the trade show, you will want to capture the names of the visitors to your booth. As we mentioned, you also want them to give enough information about themselves to decide if they are truly qualified inquiries.

Some ways to encourage people to give the information you want include asking them to drop their business cards into a "fish bowl" or fill out a brief form. Any of these methods can be used in a raffle format (where a winning card or form is chosen to receive a prize). You must weigh the cost of running a contest against the benefit of increased response and the potential of less qualified leads.

Leads from suppliers

Some suppliers may do lead generating publication advertising for their products or services. Typically, they turn over the inquiries to dealers for follow-up.

Seminar and meeting attendees

Giving a presentation at a seminar or meeting is a good way to make people aware of your organisation. Many of them will ask for additional information about the product or service, if given the opportunity by means of a card on their seat or a tear-off portion of a handout. Of course, the registration list itself is a good source of names.

All organisation written materials should include an invitation to contact you for further information.

Visitor Cards

Have any visitor to your business or organisation fill out a card.

"Take-ones"

DEFINITION

Take-ones are small pads or forms that are attached to advertisements found on buses, public bulletin boards or kiosks. These forms include an invitation to request more information about a company's products or services.

Advertising specialties

These are useful items (such as pens, lighters, magnets, etc.) with a company's name, slogan, address, telephone number imprinted on them.

Sources for prospect names

There are so many sources for prospect names that it is necessary to be very clear about what types of names are most appropriate for your organisation. Understanding the characteristics of your best customers is vital.

Understanding your target customers can help you identify the best sources for new prospects and suspects in another way. You may decide to use one of the database fields to track how current customers heard about your business or organisation. The information in this field would give an indication of where to look for potential customers.

> **note** When contacting the referral name, results will be better if you indicate who referred them to you.

Below are some of the sources for prospect and suspect names that many organisations find productive:

Referrals

Present customers may be willing to suggest the names of their friends or associates who could benefit from your product or service. These names are usually more valuable than "cold" prospects because they were selected by people who know, and are satisfied with, your organisation. Similarly, the prospect will probably be receptive to (at least) listening to your offer. A recommendation coming from a friend or associate carries with it a great deal of credibility and trust.

In addition to referrals, directories and public lists are another source for prospect and suspect names. They are less valuable than referrals because they were not given to you by someone familiar with your business or organisation.

> **note** Because people or even businesses are so mobile and because it takes so long to compile and print a directory, most directories have a relatively high "error" rate.

Directories and public lists

Many organisations publish directories which can be used to construct your own list of prospects. When you add the names from a directory to your own mailing list, they are usually yours to use without any restriction. Some directories do have limitations, so check before using names.

The significant amount of time needed is one of the biggest drawbacks to manually compiling a list from directories. For example, consider the time it would take to type all (or even some) of the entries in the yellow pages. In many cases, this work has already been done by a professional list compiler, who then offers the list for rent.

Here are a few of the many directories you might want to consult:

- Telephone directories—Both yellow and white pages.

- City directories

- Business directories—Directories compiled by type of business.

- Association directories—Many associations publish directories with listings of their members.

- *The Times Top 1,000 Companies* directory

Other lists are available through public sources:

- Local governments maintain a number of different lists which may be available in your area. Contact your local council for lists compiled from any of the following sources:

    - register of electors

    - marriage licences

    - birth certificates

    - business licences

    - business loan information

- hunting or fishing licences

- fund-raisers for elected offices

- institutional lists—public schools and hospitals may also have lists of students or births

Visitor lists or customer registration forms

Many organisations use a registration device to develop lists of people who visit their facilities or participate in their programs. Retail stores in particular are known for using this technique. To build a prospect list, they invite each visitor to the store to fill out a card with his/her name and address along with any other information desired. This request for information is sometimes presented as an entry to a raffle or sweepstakes.

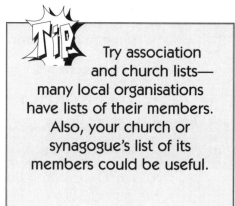

Try association and church lists— many local organisations have lists of their members. Also, your church or synagogue's list of its members could be useful.

The main thing to keep in mind is that these are many lists that are easily and inexpensively available to you, particularly if your product or service has a wide appeal within a local area.

Other options for obtaining prospect and suspect lists

When you develop prospect and suspect lists yourself, using the above sources, the names belong to you. However, compiling lists from these sources can be very time-consuming, since much of the work is manual. You may be severely limited in the number of names compiled because of the time it takes. That time restriction might also mean that when you finally complete the list, many names have moved or are no longer appropriate to mail. Also, working on your own, you may overlook (among the thousands of list sources available) those that are best for your purposes.

Several options are available to you for expanding your prospect list on a larger scale and without manually compiling the names. For example, rent or purchase names or exchange names with another organisation:

List rental

List rental can cost anywhere from £50 to more than £500 for 1,000 names. The charge is usually higher if you want to make selections within the list (for example, by business type, last order amount, etc.). Typically, 5,000 names are a minimum order quantity. However, fewer names may be rented, depending on the total size of the list.

> *note*
> Lists can be rented for one-time use only, unless otherwise agreed upon.

List owners usually include decoy names on the list to monitor the use of their lists and detect unauthorised mailings. Decoys are names that are unique to their owner's list and to each mailing. They may be "doctored" (or entirely phony) names, but they do have actual addresses. These decoys then inform the list owner when they receive a mailing with the "fake" name.

List purchase

List purchase is not as common as rental. List purchase is actually more like "long-term rental." The list is sold for permanent or long term use; that is, for some period longer than six months. The time period is usually negotiable.

> *note*
> List purchase can be a welcome option if you determine that you want to contact the names on a multiple, or unlimited, basis.

If you buy a list, you must

maintain it. In other words, you are responsible for updating names and addresses as needed, reviewing for and eliminating duplicates, and generally keeping the list in its most efficient mailable form.

note By exchanging lists you avoid the costs of list rental or list purchase. Of course, you must always take care to verify that the list you are getting is accurate, current and free of duplicates.

List exchange

As the in-house list of customers, inquiries and inactive customers grows, you may be able to exchange it with other list owners for their lists. Arrange list exchanges with organisations that have similar audiences, but do not compete directly with you. Occasionally, competitors do exchange lists for offers of a non-competitive nature.

Common types of lists available for rental, purchase or exchange

Following are examples of some of the common terms used to describe available lists:

Compiled lists

Compiled lists are prepared from names found in directories and other sources of printed (usually public) information. They are "put together" based on certain predetermined criteria such as type of business or location. When you rent a compiled list, the manual work of building a list is done for you.

Another advantage of using a compiled list is that compilers often include additional data with the list. You can often select compiled lists by such variables as age and income on a consumer list and business type and number of employees on a business list.

The disadvantages of using a compiled list are basically two-fold. You don't know how recently the list was compiled. Given the length of time it takes to compile and issue a list, the names and data could be 1 1/2 to 2 years old by the time you order and attempt to mail the list.

Also, with the exception of the possible demographic information you have about the names on the list, you have very little knowledge about whether this name has any likelihood of wanting your product or service.

Subscription lists

Subscription lists are made up of people who subscribe to a publication or a service. It is important to distinguish between paid and free subscriptions when evaluating these lists for your purposes. People who paid for a subscription are considered to be better potential responders than those who request and receive a free subscription. Subscribers might not have the same propensity to buy by mail as do names on a response list. However, based on the publications they subscribe to you know more about the names (and their interests) than you do with a compiled list.

Response lists

The names on a response list already responded to some sort of offer (from another organisation) and are thus considered more valuable. The theory is if they responded once, they are more likely to do so again!

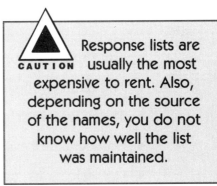
Response lists are usually the most expensive to rent. Also, depending on the source of the names, you do not know how well the list was maintained.

Below are terms commonly used to describe the names within a list:

- **Buyers:** People who made a purchase at some time.

- **Active Buyers:** Individuals on a list who more recently (usually within the last 12 months) demonstrated some form of action, e.g. purchase, rent, subscribe to a service, etc.

- **Hotline Names:** The most recent names added to a list. These names should not be older than three months and might be able to be selected by categories as recent as 30 or 60 days. If this selection is available on a list (usually at an additional charge), it is wise to consider testing it since these individuals recently demonstrated some action and their address is probably correct.

- **Inactive Buyers:** Those who purchased, but not within the last 12 months. Be careful here: These names age. Unless the list has been cleaned recently, you may get many obsolete addresses.

- **Multibuyers:** Individuals who made more than one purchase. Multibuyers, if available on a list, are the best selection to make when renting a list.

- **Inquiries:** Names who inquired, but not yet purchased. The ages of these names are very important.

Data cards

Data cards provide basic information about rental lists.

- The price of renting or purchasing the list
- The number of names available
- The different list segments available
- Hotline names available monthly or quarterly
- List selections (and the costs of those selections) for better targeting. Typical selections include:
  - Sex
  - Geographical (by post code)
  - Home vs. business address
  - Type of business

- • "Nth" name to ensure randomness for a test mailing

- • Specific name/title within the business to get the mailing (particularly if mailing to larger businesses)

- ◆ Minimum order size

- ◆ Date data card was updated

- ◆ Written description of the list

- ◆ Terms of renting or purchasing list

- ◆ Formats (and changes) for how the list is available, e.g. computer tape, microcomputer disk, Cheshire labels, peel-off labels

- ◆ Profile of the list, usually including the following:

  - • Average order size (unit of sale)

  - • Sex (% male, % female)

  - • Source of names (direct mail, membership, publication advertising, telemarketing, television and radio advertising)

  - • Method of payment (% cash buyers, % credit card buyers on the list)

- ◆ Name and address of the list manager or broker

Where to go to rent, purchase or exchange lists

There are list professionals available to help you carry out the transactions described above. In addition to handling the details of each arrangement, some may be able to advise you on which list(s) will be most effective for your purposes. Two types of list professionals—list compilers and list brokers—are described below:

List compilers

List compilers offer catalogues of the lists they built, using many of the same sources we presented above. The lists may be either compiled or response lists. The list compiler not only builds, but must maintain, the lists as well.

note It may ultimately be more efficient to use an "expert" who has already built the list you want, as long as you are prepared to purchase the names in volume.

List compilers offer literally thousands of business lists and consumer lists. The consumers on the lists range from purchasers of home burglar alarms to people who travelled to the Far East in the past three months to businesspeople in Scotland. New lists are made available regularly and are promoted through announcements and advertisements in direct marketing industry publications.

If compiled lists are appropriate for you, there are a number of sources for obtaining them. If you are seeking lists that are national in scope, the best place to begin your search is through the: Direct Marketing Association. Their address is: Haymarket House, 1 Oxendon Street, London SW1Y 4EE, tel 020 7321 2525 or 0345 034599.

List brokers

List brokers are the direct marketing field's mailing list specialists. They are independent agents whose primary function is to arrange the rental transaction between list users and list owners and compilers. List brokers must keep up-to-date with what is happening in the field in order to recommend the best selection of lists to achieve their clients' (the users) objectives.

The broker is paid a commission by the list owner. That commission is typically 20 percent of the list price. The broker collects the full amount of the list rental fees, deducts his commission and gives the balance to the list owner.

Some clients use brokers simply to order the lists. Others tap the broker's know-how about maintaining lists, keeping direct mail records and testing, as well as the creative aspects of direct marketing.

Full service agency

Another source to go to for arranging a mailing list transaction is the full service agency, which can provide the entire range of mailing function necessary to conduct a program. The agency can help select names, design and produce the mailing package, and carry out or arrange for the physical mailing. They can also arrange to have the orders filled, if necessary.

note From freelancers to direct response advertising agencies to full service advertising agencies, every imaginable service is available.

For a list of full service agencies, contact your local direct marketing associations or clubs, or consult the Yellow Pages under "Advertising—Direct Mail."

How to order a mailing list

The steps involved in ordering a mailing list may vary depending on the source used and the type of list you want to obtain. Here are some general guidelines that apply to most situations:

- Plan your list selections well in advance of a mailing. Allow at least two to four weeks for ordering and delivery of the names, as well as time for the list owner to approve the order.

- Be specific about the selections. All instructions should be written and complete.

- Specify the format you want to receive the names—computer tape, microcomputer disk, peel-off labels, hard copy, etc.

- Communicate the mailing date. If you foresee a problem in meeting it, let the list broker know as soon as possible. Also, determine whether the lists are to be delivered to you or the mailer. Specifically indicate all dates when and places where the list or computer tapes need to be delivered for each step in the processing of your mailing.

- Work closely from the start with all parties involved in the list transaction.

A good source to contact to find out more about list transactions is the Direct Marketing Association (DMA). The Direct Marketing Association is the national trade association representing both direct marketing users (such as mail-order businesses, charitable organisation, and financial institutions) and suppliers (such as list professionals, advertising agencies and printers). The Direct Marketing Association offers a wide range of services, seminars, reference books and directories on all aspects of direct marketing.

note Successful promotion to inquiry, prospect and suspect lists is the key to keeping the current customer list growing and productive. This report has outlined the various avenues available to you in the search for these potential customer lists. Your organisation may want to handle the whole effort in-house. Or, you may want to use the services of direct mail industry professionals for some or all of the steps.

Where to find the database for your customer mailing list

In-house sources

Before you think about a list of prospective customer names, you should first create a database for current customers' names and develop a mailing list. However, don't forget that if you are going to store customer information on a computer, you must have registered with the Data Protection Registrar This government body provides guidance on the laws governing the holding and using of personal data. For further details, contact them at: Wycliffe House, Water Lane, Wilmslow, Cheshire, SK9 5AF. Tel: 01625 545700.

Finding the data to include on the customer portion of your mailing list can be fairly straightforward if you have your own in-house records. Even then you may have to develop more sources to obtain additional data about your customers.

Here are some of the in-house records you can use to develop your customer database:

- **Sales Receipts/Invoices/ Order Forms:** These documents can give you the following information: date of last purchase, dates of all purchases over a period of time, and amount of money spent with you. You may also be able to determine what products/services were ordered from you. When using invoices to compile your customer list, be aware that in businesses they may be addressed to the Accounting Department rather than the individual/title most likely to purchase from you.

- **Shipping Records:** Shipping records can be an important source of customer names, particularly if your product is sold through a dealer or distributor, and you don't have direct access to customer order forms. Again, be aware that some customers may have different billing and shipping addresses.

- **Membership Lists:** Every organisation is sure to have a list of its members. If your organisation has several membership categories, this information should be associated with the member name when you add it to your list.

- **Registration Forms:** If your organisation does not maintain a membership list, you may still be able to identify your customers from the registration forms and sign-in sheets you use at your events. One approach to collecting names is to ask attendees to add their names to your mailing list.

- **Contest Entries:** The entry forms for a sweepstakes, contest, or raffle can be used effectively to get the names of

> ⚠ **CAUTION** Especially if your customers are businesses, they may use two addresses. One is the "Delivery" address, where ordered items are sent. The other is the "Invoice" or postal address, where invoices and catalogues are sent. Make sure you're using the correct address every time you correspond with the customer.

your customers. This approach might be most useful if your organisation lacks customer records because you provide your product or service free of charge.

Other sources

Sometimes, your own records don't hold enough information about your customers or members. You may have to rely on other sources to capture additional database information:

- ◆ **Warranty Cards:** Warranty cards included in packages of merchandise can be an effective way to gather information about customers. On the card, you can request that the customer complete the demographic information and return it when he/she registers the product.

◆ **Surveys:** Phone or mail surveys are another way to gather (and later update) information on your customer database.

Phone surveys can be used in a number of different ways to collect database information. For example, you can call customers and administer full questionnaires to gather complete information about them. This can be a very costly way to collect data—especially for a large number of customers. Mail surveys (which will be discussed later) may be a better technique for this type of database information collection.

Mail questionnaires can reach a larger number of customers at a lower cost than phone surveys. Mail questionnaires can be sent individually to customers. However, to save postage costs, surveys can also be inserted in mailings, included in packages of merchandise, or printed on any other correspondence with customers, such as invoices.

If you have a store or office, you can also conduct surveys by having customers fill out questionnaire cards when they visit.

Other sources you can use to build your list include:

- point-of-purchase questionnaires

- membership application forms

- questions on purchase orders, statements, invoices

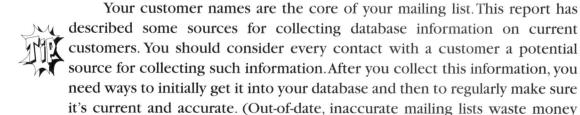

Your customer names are the core of your mailing list. This report has described some sources for collecting database information on current customers. You should consider every contact with a customer a potential source for collecting such information. After you collect this information, you need ways to initially get it into your database and then to regularly make sure it's current and accurate. (Out-of-date, inaccurate mailing lists waste money and reduce results.)

Compile, maintain and sell "red hot" name lists

10

Chapter 10

Compile, maintain and sell "red hot" name lists

What you'll find in this chapter:

⟹ When a list is not right for you

⟹ How much should a list cost?

⟹ Compile your own list

⟹ The function of list brokers

⟹ How to test a list

The mailing list

Virtually every inquiry or buyer's name ultimately ends up on a mailing list. Some are small lists, while others contain millions of names. Some are meticulously maintained, while others are carelessly handled.

note For those interested in mail-order advertising, mailing lists can prove to be very valuable as well as a saleable commodity.

If you wish to increase your sales, it is often a good idea to go into direct mail. To do this you begin by renting another firm's mailing lists. Or, you rent your list of customers' names to another firm. Either way, mailing lists play an important part in the everyday world of mail-order.

Basically, there are three types of lists. They are:

- house lists

- mail response lists

- compiled lists

House lists

DEFINITION

A *house list* is a list of your own customers. They may be active or inactive. They may be inquiries or buyers. They may have made ten purchases or just one, or in the case of inquiries, none. They may have placed an order in the last four months, or in the last four years. They may have spent a great deal of money or a small amount. They may be credit card buyers or cash buyers.

> *note*
>
> You can spend a great deal of money to rent outside lists, but none will bring you the financial rewards you will reap from your own customer list.

Your house list contains your most valuable asset—the names of your own customers. These are the people who purchased from you in the past and are likely to purchase from you in the future. These people know and trust you, and will order on a continuing basis.

Mail response lists

DEFINITION

Second in importance are *mail response* lists. These are people who responded to another firm's direct mail offer. The idea is to pick out a list of customers who ordered products similar to those sold by your firm. Since it is a well-known fact that these people previously responded to an offer similar to yours, there is an excellent chance that they will also respond favourably to your offer.

Compiled lists

Although the people on compiled lists do not usually respond as well as the people on house lists or mail response lists, these lists can still be helpful if properly used. These lists are not generally used by small or medium

I never used a compiled list and do not recommend their use for anyone but the largest mailers.

sized business firms because they are too general in nature. But large firms, such as oil companies and insurance firms, find them useful and even profitable.

While there are no set rules that can be applied to mailing lists, here are few "rules of thumb" that can be regarded as reliable in most cases. They may not apply to your list situation, but they give you food for thought.

- The average list changes at least 15%-20% each year. Some mailing lists change only 10%, while others have as high as a 100% rate of turnover. (Lists of university graduates, etc.)

- A direct response list (people who already purchased goods through the mail) will out-pull a compiled list.

- A customer list will out-pull all other outside lists (direct response or compiled lists).

- Allocate 10% or more of your direct mail budget to list development and maintenance. The 10% figure is the minimum amount you should spend. Most successful businesses find the more they spend the more they prosper.

- People over 35 years of age as a group respond to mail-order offers at a much higher rate than do younger people.

- People living in rural areas respond to mail-order offers at a higher rate than do people who live in urban areas.

- People who ordered through the mail within the last 3 - 6 months ("hot-line" buyers) are the most productive names you can get.

- Multiple buyers (people who made two or more separate purchases through the mail within a season) will always outpull buyers who purchased only once within a season.

- The results you can expect will vary by season and/or months of the year, and by regional area.

- Every list should be checked and cleaned at least twice a year or more. It is a good idea to review and update your list at least every six months whenever possible.

 Use outside consultants and service organisations to help you with your list decision. These people made it their business to study and understand lists.

Responsibility for maintaining and updating of your list should be delegated to a single individual whenever possible. You've heard the expression "too many cooks spoil the broth." Well, when it comes to mailing lists, it is a good idea to limit the number of individuals who handle the list to as few as is possible. The fewer the better.

Should you use lists?

The first thing to consider when trying to make a decision about a particular list is whether or not the people on that list would be interested in your product. You want a list of people that purchased something similar to your product, or at least something in the same general category. People who already purchased cheese products are perfect for you if you are selling cheese products. But, if you are selling fishing supplies you would never want to rent a list of buyers interested in cheese products. Instead, you would want to rent a list of people interested in fishing. You might consider renting a list of names from a publisher that publishes a fishing magazine. Or maybe, a list of people who recently applied for a fishing license.

What to spend

TIP

When renting lists, it is imperative to find a list that parallels as closely as possible your own list of customers. The right list usually makes a tremendous difference in the results you can expect.

Today, there are thousands of mailing lists available in thousands of categories. Almost any offer, no matter how unusual, can be matched to an appropriate list. The price of a mailing list can start from as low as £50 per thousand to as high as £1000 per thousand and more. A few of the factors that determine the price of a mailing list are:

- freshness of list

- buyer or inquiry

- amount of purchase

- multiple or one time buyer

- "hot-line" buyers

- credit card buyers

- frequency of purchase

- brokers recommend its use

note

As you can see, many factors come into play when pricing a mailing list. The more desirable the list, the more you can expect to pay.

Name lists—a profit centre for you

Many companies with as few as a few thousand names are earning a substantial income from the rental of their list. Larger firms who have lists in excess of 50,000 names are reaping huge rewards. If you simply bear in mind the fact that these small companies with small lists are able to gross £40,000 a year and more in rental income fees alone, you begin to grasp a measure of the significance of just how profitable the buying and selling of names can be for you. It is truly a profit centre without parallel in the mail-order industry.

List prices depend on the time and money you spend compiling them. Some lists are easily accessible and you cannot charge a great deal for them. Other lists require a great deal of time and money to compile. These lists are usually very expensive.

 You have probably seen many dealers advertising their lists at cut-rate prices. In most cases these lists are worthless or so out-of-date that they are no longer of any use to anyone, except to sell to unsuspecting mail-order buyers. Try to stay away from these dealers. Most of them are selling rubbish.

note It is not uncommon for many mail-order businesses to make more money from the rental of their lists than they earn from the rest of their business.

Your own list

Once you get your mail-order business off the ground and have a large enough list of inquiries or buyers, or both, it is a good idea to put your customer list up for rental with as many brokers as possible.

While it is true that the primary purpose of compiling your own list of customers is to generate sales of your own products, an important secondary source of income can be generated through the rental of your list to non-competing firms. Profits from the rental of house lists can be enormous. Indeed, if it were not for the monies received from list rentals, many a mail-order firm would soon be forced to go out of business.

For example, let us assume that you have a customer list of 50,000 names. This list is considered small by most experts, but it still accounts for hefty revenues. If you charge £40 per thousand names, you receive £2,000 each time you rent your list. Of course, you have to allow for the brokers commission of 20% or £400. That still leaves you with £1,600, assuming there are no other costs involved. If you rent your list ten times during the course of a year you should net approximately £6,000.

> *note* Some firms take a middle-of-the-road approach to the renting of their list. These firms make sure they rent only their old subscribers list or inactive customer list. They do not rent their current subscribers list or the names of their active customers.

Another benefit of renting your list to non-competing firms is that you are able to get new ideas and insights about what your customers' likes and dislikes are. In addition, one of the firms that rents your list may try an approach that you might want to imitate.

Many firms refuse to rent their house list to another firm. They feel that the results of their future mailings will be diluted if their customers are deluged with offers from other companies. Other firms feel just the opposite is true. They state that as long as they rent their list to a non-competing firm no harm is done. In fact, many feel that by renting their list to other companies, they are helping to insure that their customers continue to be mail-order buyers.

Finally, there are the firms that exchange lists with both their competitors and non-competitors. Usually, only inquiries of inactive customers names are swapped. The best part of list swapping is the cost. If you normally pay £40 per thousand names for a list, you can get it for only £8 per thousand names when you swap lists. (You pay only the brokers fee, or 20% of £40.)

Functions of list brokers

The Direct Mail Association research report lists the most important services performed by list brokers.

Finds new lists—The broker is constantly seeking new lists and selecting for your consideration ones that will be of particular interest. In fact, brokers spend a great deal of their time encouraging list owners to enter the list rental field.

Checks the names against MPS (Mailing Preference Service)—Recognised brokers obey a standard code of practice and always check their lists against the latest information held by MPS. This way, keeping to the law is their responsibility - not yours.

Acts as a clearing house for data—The broker saves you valuable time because you can go to one source for a considerable amount of information, rather than to many sources which may or may not be readily available.

Screens information—The broker carefully screens the list information provided by the list owner. Where possible he or one of his representatives personally verifies the information provided by the list owner.

Advises on testing—The broker's knowledge of the makeup of a list is often valuable in determining what will constitute a representative cross section of the list. Obviously, an error in selecting a cross section will invalidate the results of the test and possibly eliminate from your schedule a group of names that could be responsive.

Checks instructions—When you place an order with a list owner through a broker, he and his staff double check the accuracy and completeness of your instructions, thus often avoiding unnecessary misunderstandings and loss of time.

Clears offer—The broker clears for you in advance the mailing you wish to make. He supplies the list owner either with a sample of your piece or a description of it, and by getting prior approval minimises the chance of any later disappointments.

Checks mechanics—The broker clears with the list owner the particular type of envelope, order card, or other material which is to be addressed.

Clears mailing date—When contacting the list owner, the broker checks on the mailing date which you request and asks that it be held open as a protected time for you.

Works out timing—The broker arranges either for material to be addressed or labels to be sent to you at a specified time, thus enabling you to maintain your schedule of inserting and mailing.

List owner-broker relations

Get list maintenance advice—Consult with the list broker when deciding how to maintain your list so you may set it up the most practical, economical and rentable way.

note If a list contains a percentage of names of people who bought on open account and failed to pay, give this information to the broker.

Discuss rates—Discuss with your broker the price you will charge for rentals and decide on a price schedule that will bring you the greatest volume of profitable business.

Supply accurate data—Be sure the list information you furnish is accurate. If the addresses in a list were not corrected within a reasonable period of time, tell the broker.

If you represent your list as made up entirely of buyers, be sure it does not include any inquiry or prospect names.

If you bought out a competitor and included some of their names in your customer list, be sure to state this fact. Aside from obvious aspects of misrepresentation, you are the one who suffers when you mislead a broker.

Address on schedule—Establish a reputation for addressing on time as promised. If you accept orders and fail to fulfil them on schedule, brokers become aware of this and find they cannot conscientiously suggest your list to potential users. If, for some reason, you foresee a delay, advise the broker immediately, so he can advise the mailer.

Furnish latest counts—Keep the broker posted on current list counts, rates, changes in the sources of the names and the like. When the composition of a list changes, it may very well become more interesting to a user who previously felt that it was not suitable for his purpose. In addition, when current information is offered to a potential user through the broker, it is more likely to develop activity than is an out-dated description.

Choose brokers wisely—Consider carefully whether to make your list available to a number of list brokers or just to one broker. There are many things to be said in favour of working with several brokers. At times, there are also some good reasons for working exclusively with one broker. While the decision is yours, you should keep in mind the fact that brokers are people and each has his own particular personality, following, and sphere of influence. Therefore, as a list owner, you are well advised not to narrow the field unless your facilities for addressing are so limited that the orders one broker develop for you are more than sufficient to take up all the available addressing time.

> **note** The broker is a member of your sales force. Your broker can only continue to do an effective job so long as you protect him on the accounts he develops for you.

Protect brokers—It takes a lot of time and effort on the part of a broker to interest a mailer in testing your list. Therefore, continuation runs should be scheduled through the original broker so long as he continues to render satisfactory service to his client.

Recently there has been a trend toward list management as opposed to list brokers. A list manager takes over complete management of your list for rental purposes. Under this form of contract, the list manager is responsible for the following functions:

- He solicits his own brokerage customers directly.

- Makes all contacts with list brokers and is responsible for processing their orders.

- Should, at his own expense, advertise the list.

- Analyses the results of each mailing and offers suggestions and advice.

- Keeps all records and is responsible for all billings.

- Provides the list owner with a detailed list of activity, along with commissions earned, etc.

> **note** It is not unusual for a good list manager to double or even triple your previous rental income. Naturally, some list managers do a better job than others.

For this extra service, he usually earns an additional 10%. Today, however, many list managers ask for and get more. In my opinion, they are worth the extra money. A good list manager does the utmost to promote your list. In return, the list manager earns a substantial sum of money. But, not as much as the list owner. If you decide to use a list manger instead of a broker, select the best one available. It takes some time, but it is time well spent.

I strongly suggest you subscribe to one of the following magazines: *Marketing Week*, tel: 020 7970 4000; the monthly publication *Direct Response*, tel: 020 7917 5726; or *Interactive Marketing*, available bi-monthly from all good newsagents. Any of these will keep you abreast of the latest information available dealing with direct marketing and list selection.

How to test a list

Today the minimum number of names you are allowed to test is usually around 5,000. However, many brokers waive this rule. They do not want to lose a potentially good customer just because he or she wants to test 3,000 names instead of 5,000.

When testing a list always request Nth selection. This ensures that you are testing the effectiveness of the entire list, and not just one small segment. Nth selection simply means that the computer randomly picks a few names from the entire list. The reason you should always use Nth selection is simple, besides the obvious reason already mentioned. It stops the broker or list owner from giving you his loaded names. Many a shrewd broker or list owner will rent you only their best names when you test a list. This ensures that you get the best results possible. Later, when you return for additional names, you get the shock of your life.

In order for a beginner to get a trustworthy list, it might be a good idea to rent your first list from a large, reputable firm. Later, as you grow, tests can be made with lists from smaller firms. Another reason for selecting larger lists is that, should the results be rewarding, you have a larger selection of names for your future use.

Always try to rent a list consisting of buyers' names only. The more recent the better. If you cannot get a list of buyers' names only, go for a mixed list. This particular list will consist of both buyers' and inquiries' names. Once again, it is advisable to get the freshest names possible.

Always make certain that any list you decide to rent was cleaned within the last 6-12 months. Otherwise, you may be throwing your time and money away.

Who buys mailing lists

All mail-order experts agree that there is no less expensive way to increase their sales than by using the medium of direct mail. The problem all direct mail users face is where can they obtain the lists they need to continue their mailing campaigns. That is where the "mailing list dealer" comes in. By being able to supply these firms with names of authentic mail-order prospects, he or she is able to build a very successful business.

Lists that are not CAUTION kept up-to-date deteriorate rapidly. Many lists are totally worthless unless they are constantly cleaned.

Once a firm has faith in you and the list you furnish, you can be assured that they will continue to use your service as long as you give them the same excellent service and results as in the beginning. Remember, the compiling and selling of names is a very competitive business. Yet, many aspirants, most with little or no knowledge of the business, strike it rich in this field. You must at all times offer your clients top-notch service and order-pulling lists.

How to get started

The starting supplies needed to operate a mailing list business are moderate and inexpensive. You'll definitely need a typewriter (the best one you can possibly afford). Additionally, you'll need the following supplies: letterheads and envelopes; business cards; record books; some sort of filing cabinet; sheets of perforated gummed label (available at most stationery stores); carbon paper, shipping envelopes or containers; pens and pencils and a few other supplies as you start to grow.

There are two ways for beginners to compile name lists: (1) On standard gummed labels, (2) Computer labels, from a home computer or a large main frame computer, (available from firms who specialise in this field). Since this book is primarily for beginners we first discuss the gummed labels. Later in this book, there is a section devoted to computer lists.

Mailing lists are usually typed on sheets of perforated gummed labels ready to affix to envelopes. These standard sheets of perforated gummed labels come in various pack sizes, 250 per pack, for example, with a cost of around £5.00 per pack. You can also offer the customer name lists on plain bond paper, usually there are from 35-

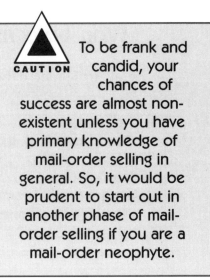

To be frank and candid, your chances of success are almost non-existent unless you have primary knowledge of mail-order selling in general. So, it would be prudent to start out in another phase of mail-order selling if you are a mail-order neophyte.

60 names typed on a plain piece of paper. I do not generally recommend this method of name selling since it usually indicates the seller is a rank amateur.

note

Another method of reproduction of your mailing list is a copy machine. You simply insert your master copy into the machine and copy as many sheets as you need. You can do this for pressure sensitive labels as well as gummed labels. If you can afford to rent, lease or buy your own copy machine it will greatly increase your volume and also your profit potential.

There are many, many people using the above methods to reproduce and sell their name lists. Many are making a small fortune. But, the real big money cannot be made until you computerise your list.

note

As you expand, you will want to use a method that allows you to put the names in exact postal code order. This is a very important factor when selling your list of names. In the beginning, you will not have the experience or money needed to properly organise your list.

Computerise your mailing list for greater profits

Probably the one question most frequently asked by mail-order list compilers is, "should I or shouldn't I computerise my list?" The answer is, "that depends." There are many factors to be considered before you make up your mind one way or the other. One thing is for sure, if computerising your list is right for you, it will improve your profit potential in two ways. (1) By a more efficient marketing of your list (2) By increasing your income from the rental of your list.

> **note** If you plan on increasing the size and profitability of your list, computerising your list isn't only desirable, it's virtually indispensable.

Until recently, it was not a good idea to computerise your list if it contained fewer than 15,000-20,000 names. Today, however, with the aid of small office and home computers, anyone can easily store and print out a large amount of names.

If you do decide to enter data into a computer, you must register as a data user with the Data Protection Registrar and comply with the terms of the Data Protection Act. Luckily, this isn't as hard as it sounds - just call the DPR on 01625 545700. They'll provide you with a full copy of the regulations.

How to clean your list

You clean your list by putting the caption "address correction requested" in the upper left hand corner of your outer envelope when you mail to your own list. Or, you can offer your customers 10 new names for every one old name they return to you. This way you do not have to send out any mailings yourself. Your customers clean the list for you.

List maintenance is principally a matter of adding new names, deleting "nixies" (undeliverable mail) and entering changes of address as customers move. None of these tasks are difficult, but without the proper care and dedication a good list can soon become worthless.

> *note*
>
> Remember, computerised lists are like children. You have to maintain them after you bring them into the world.

Where to obtain names for your list

Naturally, you can rent out your own list of customers if you have such a list. This is the way most beginners start. We previously discussed this aspect of name rentals. You can also compile other types of name lists. Examples— doctors, solicitors, chemists, secondary school students, etc. Several books and directories are published that specifically deal with these types of lists. Two of the best are *The Complete Direct Mail List Handbook,* and *Secrets of Successful Direct Marketing.* These books are not cheap, so if you do not wish to buy them, they are available at most large public libraries.

Another method of compiling names for a name list is to purchase the names from a mail-order dealer. The price you offer for these names is usually just a fraction of what they would cost if you paid for the advertisements. I know of one list compiler who became a very rich man using this method. He sends a form letter to mail-order dealers who advertise in the classified sections of magazines. He offers to buy their current names and all their names in the future for a fair price. After he acquires the names, he has them put on a computer listing and sells them to some of the biggest mail-order firms in the country. He has done this for a long time and is the king of the opportunity-seekers name list market.

What prices to charge

Always remember to keep your list prices in line with what the other list sellers are charging. If you charge too little, most people will shy away, figuring that your list is not that good. On the other hand, if you set your price too high, most prospects will be financially unable or unwilling to spend too great a sum of money. Always try to be moderate in your price structure. If you are having good results renting your list, you might try raising the price slowly and see what happens. Never jump your price too rapidly if at all possible. This tends to scare away many good prospects and old customers.

How to advertise

There are many and varied methods of reaching prospective buyers of your lists. We will discuss a few in this chapter. Remember, there are literally dozens of other ways to reach customers. We cannot and will not cover all the methods, but we attempt to cover some of the most widely used methods.

note Many advertisers use classified ads because they are cheap and yet reach a very large audience.

Advertise in various trade and business publications. There are magazines like *Marketing Week* that list dozens of mailing lists in each issue. These ads are usually placed by the list broker, list manager or the list owner. This is probably the best method to use if you are going after big results. It costs a little, but it is well worth the price. You can also advertise your list in business opportunity magazines and periodicals. There are hundreds of these publications available for you to choose from. You have to test to see which one works the best for you.

You can place classified ads in magazines. Never ask for money directly from a classified ad. These ads should be used only to solicit inquiries. When you receive the prospective buyer's inquiry, you send them all the relative information about your list. Another very profitable method used by list sellers is to rent a list of prospective buyers from another seller. Once you attain this list, you mail out your list information to this list.

EXAMPLE: If you are selling a list containing the names of people who inquired about a book on weight-watching, you might try to rent a list of names from another dealer who is selling a book dealing with the same subject. You would ask the other dealer to send you a list of all the people who rented his list. Since they rented his list of people interested in weight-watching, there is a good chance they would be interested in renting a similar list from you.

Protect your lists

If a mailer rents your list and is not specifically given permission to mail to it more than one time, and does so, then he is guilty of fraud. The best way to catch anyone doing this is to seed your list. Put the names and addresses of about a dozen people in the list and alert them to inform you if they receive more than one mail offer from the same person or firm. The fact that they do so does not automatically mean that you were defrauded. As you learned from the information presented, it is highly probable that the name is on more than one list. It is worth investigating though and I would investigate before filing any formal charges.

> *note*
> It is a fact of life that no one will want to help you if he thinks you are trying to take the food out of their family's mouths. It is no different in the list selling and compiling field.

The best way to prevent multiple mailings is to include a letter with the name list informing the renter that the list is seeded and threaten prosecution for misuse. Such a letter will cause an unscrupulous person to have second thoughts about taking liberties with your list.

Get help from the experts

If you need to, call some of the biggest names in the mailing list business and tell them you are interested in having your list of names managed by them. Tell them that your list contained 50,000 buyers of mail-order books. As you discuss your list, ask a few off-the-cuff questions that you need answered.

note

Since they were interested in managing your list, they would only be too glad to answer any and all of your questions. You might say that this method is sneaky and not above board. I would say that I did what I had to do to increase my knowledge of the mailing list business.

Appendix

100 words that have sales appeal

Add sale punch to describe your merchandise or sales offer—use one of the following words. It may be helpful used alone or with other words. They have been selected from successful ads for convenience in preparing your copy.

Absolutely	Fascinating	Miracle	Sensational
Amazing	Fortune	Noted	Simplified
Approved	Full	Odd	Sizable
Attractive	Genuine	Outstanding	Special
Authentic	Gift	Personalised	Startling
Bargain	Gigantic	Popular	Strange
Beautiful	Greatest	Powerful	Strong
Better	Guaranteed	Practical	Sturdy
Big	Helpful	Professional	Successful
Colourful	Highest	Profitable	Superior
Colossal	Huge	Profusely	Surprise
Complete	Immediately	Proven	Terrific
Confidential	Improved	Quality	Tested
Crammed	Informative	Quickly	Tremendous
Delivered	Instructive	Rare	Unconditional
Direct	Interesting	Reduced	Unique
Discount	Largest	Refundable	Unlimited
Easily	Latest	Remarkable	Unparalleled
Endorsed	Lavishly	Reliable	Unsurpassed
Enormous	Liberal	Revealing	Unusual
Excellent	Lifetime	Revolutionary	Useful
Exciting	Limited	Scarce	Valuable
Exclusive	Lowest	Secrets	Wealth
Expert	Magic	Security	Weird
Famous	Mammoth	Selected	Wonderful

65 phrases stimulating action

Close your ad with an action-getting phrase. Give the reader something to write or do. Here are 65 suggestions for ways to get action. Study them. They will help you prepare your copy for better results.

Act now!
Send your name
All sent free to introduce
Amazing literature . . . Free
Ask for free folder
Bargain lists sent free
Be first to qualify
Booklet free!
Catalogue included free
Complete details free
Current list free
Dealers write for prices
Description sent free
Details free!
Everything supplied!
Exciting details free
Extra for promptness
First lesson free
Folder free!
For literature, write:
Free booklet explains
Free plans tell how
Free selling kit
Free wholesale plan
Free with approvals
Full particulars free
Get facts that help
Get started today!
Get your copy now!
Get yours wholesale
Gifts with purchases
Illustrated lists free
interesting details free
Investigate today
It's Free! . . . Act Now!.
Literature free

Mail material to:
Money making facts free
No obligation! Write!
Offer limited!
Send today
Order direct from:
Order Now!
Don't Delay!
Particulars free
Postcard brings details
Request free literature
Revealing booklet free
Rush name for details
Sales kit furnished
Sample details free
Samples sent on trial
See before you buy
Send for free details
Send for it today
Send no money
Send post card today
Send today
Send your want lists
Stamp brings details
Stamped envelope brings
Test lesson free
Unique sample offer
Valuable details free
Write for free booklet free
Write us first!
Yours for the asking

Useful addresses

Advertising Association (AA)
Abford House
15 Wilton Road
London SW1V 1NJ
Tel: 020 7828 2771

**The Advertising Standards Authority
(ASA)**
Brook House
2 - 16 Torrington Place
London WC1E 7HN
Tel: 020 7580 5555

Audit Bureau of Circulations
Black Prince Yard
207 High Street
Berkhamsted, Herts
HP4 1AD
Tel: 01442 870 800

**British Association of
Printers & Copy Centre Ltd**
76 Berwick Street
London W1V
Tel: 020 7734 7766

**British Code of Advertising Practice
(BCAP)**
Committee of Advertising Practice
Brook House
2 -16 Torrington Place
London WC1E 7HN
Tel: 020 7580 5555

British Market Research Bureau
53 The Mall
London W5 3TE
Tel: 020 8567 3060

**British Printing Industries
Federation**
11 Bedford Row
London WC1R 4DX
Tel: 020 7242 6904

**British Promotional Merchandise
Association (BMPA)**
Bank Chambers
15 High Road
Byfleet, Surrey
KT14 7QH
Tel: 01932 355 660/1

British Rate & Data (BRAD)
Maclean Hunter Ltd - publishers
Maclean House
Chalk Lane
Cockfosters Road
Barnet, Herts
EN4 0BU
Tel: 020 8975 9759

British Toy and Hobby Association
80 Camberwell Road
London SE5
Tel: 020 7701 7271

Data Protection Registrar
Wycliffe House
Water Lane
Wilmslow, Cheshire
SK9 5AF
Tel: 01625 545 745

Direct Mail Information Service
5 Carlisle Street
London
W1V 5RG
Tel:020 7494 0483

Direct Marketing Association UK Ltd
Haymarket House
1 Oxendon Street
London SW1Y 4EE
Tel: 020 7321 2525 or 0345 034599

Direct Mail Accreditation and Recognition Centre (DMARC)
248 Tottenham Court Road
London W1P 9AD
Tel: 020 7631 0904

Direct Response
64 Charlotte Street
London W1P 1LR
Tel: 020 7637 7931

Direct Selling Association
29 Floral Street
London WC2E
Tel: 020 7497 1234

Directory Publishers Association
93A Blenheim Crescent
London W11 2EQ
Tel: 020 7221 9089

Federation of Small Businesses
2 Catherine Place
London SW1E
Tel: 020 7233 7900

Institute of Direct Marketing
1 Park Road
Teddington, Middx
TW11 0AR
Tel: 020 8977 5705

The Leaflet Company
1 Hind Court
149 Fleet Street
London EC4A 3DL
Tel: 020 7583 2010

Mail Order Protection Scheme (MOPS)
16 Tooks Court
London EC4A 1LB
Tel: 020 7405 6806

Mail Order Traders' Association (MOTA)
40 Waterloo Road
Birkdale
Southport PR8 2NG
Tel: 01704 563 787

Mailing Preference Service
Haymarket House
1 Oxendon Street
London SW1Y 4EE
Tel: 020 7766 4410

Newspapers Publishers Association Ltd
34 Southwark Bridge Road
London SE1 9EU
Tel:020 7928 6928

Newspaper Society
Bloomsbury House
Bloomsbury Square
74 -77 Great Russell Street
London WC1B 3DA
Tel: 020 7636 7014

Periodical Publishers Association (PPA)
Queens House
28 Kingsway
London WC2B 6JR
Tel: 020 7404 4166

Royal Mail Customer Information Centre
Tel: 0345 950 950

Mail Order Catalogues:

Buyer's Choice
Hyde House
The Hyde
London NW9
Tel: 020 8200 7686

Go Star Retail Ltd
235 Regent's Park
London N3
Tel: 020 7366 4980

Nice Irma's By Post
Finchley Industrial Centre
879 High Road
London N12
Tel: 020 8343 7610

Bulk Despatch Mailers:

Herald International Mailings Ltd
Units 9 & 10
Merton Park Industrial Estate
Lee Road
London SW19 3HX
Tel: 020 8543 4087

Magazine Mailing Ltd
1 -8 Haslemere Industrial Estate
Parkwood
Maidstone ME15 9LQ
Tel: 01622 673 173

Packpost Services Ltd
Griffin House
Griffin Lane
Aylesbury
HP19 3BP
Tel: 01296 487 493

On-line Resources

Hobby Magazines:
http://gt.freeshop.com
www.magsnow.com
www.artscraftshobbies.com
www.krause.com
http://w3.one.net

Direct Mail & Marketing information:
www.greatlists.com
www.mailing-labels.co.uk

DM Resources, mailing lists, etc:
www.dmworld.com

Direct Mail:
www.paradedirect.com
www.aig.org

Ideas & Tools for Website users:
www.bhenterprises.com

Marketing Community:
www.marketinguk.co.uk
www.cashflowmarketing.com

Marketing online:
www.marketing.haynet.com

Keywords Direct:
www.keywords.co.uk

Yahoo! Mailing Lists:
http://dir.yahoo.com/Business_and_Economy/
Companies/Marketing/Direct_Marketing/Direct
_Mail/Mailing_Lists/

Lists:
www.listsnow.com/uk/uk-welcome.htm

The Office of Fair Trading:
www.oft.gov.uk

Details on MOPS:
www.ppa.co.uk

Newspapers:
www.guardian.co.uk
www.thepaperboy.com
www.telegraph.co.uk
www.cambridge-news.co.uk

Periodical Publishers Association:
www.ppa.co.uk

The Stationery Office (formerly HMSO)
www.hmso.gov.uk

Radio Authority:
www.radioauthority.gov.uk

Help and information for small businesses:
www.pjmallard.com
www.elom.com

Wholesale General Merchandise Suppliers, Directories and Sources:
www.crestco.net

Advertising information:
www.angelfire.com
www.crestco.net
www.money-at-home.com

Free advertising resources:
www.webfreebees.net

Classified Ads:
www.icemall.com
www.4-1-1.com
www.members.spree.com
www.sundaypaper.com
www.classifieds.bmi.net

Advertising Standards Authority:
www.asa.org.uk

The Advertising Association:
www.adassoc.org.uk

SOHO – Small Business Journal:
www.smalloffice.com

Federation of Small Businesses:
www.fsb.org.uk

Everything you need to know about Business – search engine:
www.bizbot.net

Business Information Zone:
www.thebiz.co.uk

Business Services:
www.fletel.co.uk
www.creditman.co.uk

Business Lists:
www.pavilion.co.uk

Business News Letters UK
www.net-profit.co.uk

Mail Order Catalogues:
www.catalogsfroma-z.com
www.catalink.co.uk
www.catexpress.com

Collectors' Catalogues:
www.petes-place.demon.co.uk
www.iann.mcmail.com
www.artefact.co
www.eder.it
www.cadvision.com
www.antiquesonline.com.au
www.csmonline.com/antiquetrader
www.celebrityconnection.com/free.htm
www.coinworld.com
http://collectors-news.com

Index

response lists **176**

testing of **186**

Mailing Preference Service (MPS) **182**

manuscript, preparation of **88**

marketing **62**

media advertising **154**

N

names

company **39**

hotline **164,179**

list, as a profit centre **180**

nixies **190**

O

Office of Fair Trading **71**

P

Patent Office **78,91**

payments **52**

phone surveys **171**

postage and shipping **51**

postal laws **78**

price claims, regulations on **73**

prime source **96-97**

print and mail dealers **138-140**

printing cost **52**

prizes and promotions **75**

products

most profitable **8**

pricing of **44**

prospecting **151-152**

R

record keeping **19,53**

referrals **158**

response lists **163**

S

short reports **98**

starting capital **41**

Stern, Alfred **43**

subscription list **163**

suppliers **44**

T

take-ones **157**

tax shelters **118**

telephone **40**

testimonials **15**

testing **18**

trade show exhibiting **155**

Trade Marks Registry **79**

two-part approach **12,128-133**

two-step system **152**